Description and Selection of Communication Services for Service Oriented Network Architectures

Rahamatullah Khondoker

Description and Selection of Communication Services for Service Oriented Network Architectures

 **Springer** Vieweg

Rahamatullah Khondoker
Darmstadt, Germany

Winner of the Competition for the Best Composite Service awarded from Ericsson Germany.
The Most Thought-Provoking Presentation awarded from Future Internet Assembly (FIA) Research Roadmap Group, Europe.
Nominated for Best Paper Awards from NoF2011 and AINTEC 2014.

ISBN 978-3-658-12741-1   ISBN 978-3-658-12742-8 (eBook)
DOI 10.1007/978-3-658-12742-8

Library of Congress Control Number: 2016931329

Springer Vieweg

Printed on acid-free paper

This Springer Vieweg imprint is published by Springer Nature
The registered company is Springer Fachmedien Wiesbaden GmbH

Dedicated to my parents

Acknowledgements

I would like to thank all of the individuals who consciously or unconsciously supported me during my doctoral research work by extending their helping hands. This document, which is the result of the research, would not have been made possible without their support and assistance.

My first emotional thank goes to my parents Abul Kashem and Rahima Khatun and my eight siblings who brought me up and educated me during my staying in Bangladesh. Without their help, I could not come to study in Germany and do my research work.

Secondly, thanks to all of my friends, family members, teachers and neighbors from whom I have been learning from my existence in the world. This document contains the knowledge that I gained from them.

I must express my special gratitude to my first supervisor Prof. Dr. Paul Müller who gave me a position in his research group [1], helped me in providing technical and financial support, and provided fruitful feedback for my research work.

---

[1] Integrated Communication Systems (ICSY), University of Kaiserslautern, Germany

I was very lucky to meet with Prof. Dr. Paul Francis [2]. Through small talks, I shared my research work with him. Thanks to Prof. Francis who agreed to be my second supervisor and provided comments and feedback during my dissertation planning and writing.

I would like to thank Dr.-Ing. Bernd Reuther, who guided me during my work in the projects G-Lab [3], G-Lab DEEP and PRUNO [4]. Moreover, his day-to-day feedback during my dissertation writing helped me in producing such a concise and less error prone document.

During my research work, the feedback from my colleagues in ICSY were really helpful. I should not forget to mention their names: Şenol Arikan, Tino Fleuren, Daniel Günther, Joachim Götze, Rawnak Hameed, Markus Hillenbrand, Aneta Kabzeva, Nathan Kerr, Dennis Schwerdel, Abbas Siddiqui, Eric MSP Veith and Michel Steichen.

Last but not least, I would like to thank my wife Eva-Marie Khondoker and my son Kaysan Yamin Khondoker for their love and sacrifice towards me especially during my dissertation writing as I could not spend many weekends with them.

---

[2] Director, Max Plank Institute for Software Systems (MPI-SWS)

[3] G-Lab, sponsored by the Federal Ministry of Education and Research, Germany

[4] PRUNO is funded within Call 5 of the Network of Excellence Euro-NF as Specific Joint Research Project (SJRP)

Contents

List of Figures

List of Tables

Acronyms

ADAPTIVE A Dynamically Assembled Protocol Transformation, Integration and eValuation Environment

ACD ADAPTIVE communication descriptors

AES Advanced Encryption Standard

AHP Analytic Hierarchy Process

ALS MPEG-4 Audio Lossless Coding

ANA Autonomic Network Architecture

API Application Programming Interface

ARP Address Resolution Protocol

ARQ Automatic Repeat-reQuest

ARPANET Advanced Research Projects Agency network

BB Building Block

BER Bit error rate

BGP Border Gateway Protocol

BPEL Business Process Execution Languages

CI Consistency Index

CPC Cartesian Perceptual Compression

CR Consistency Ratio

CRC   Cyclic Redundancy Check

CSDL   Communication Service Description Language

CSMA/CD   Carrier Sense Multiple Access with Collision Detection

DaCaPo   Dynamic Configuration of Protocols

DES   Data Encryption Standard

DML   Data Manipulation Language

DNS   Domain Name System

DoS   Denial of Service

DSD   Data Synchronization and Delivery

EDGE   Enhanced Data rates for GSM Evolution

ELECTRE   ELimination and Choice Expressing REality

EVAMIX   Evaluation of Mixed Criteria

FCSS   Function Based Communication Subsystem

FEC   Forward Error Correction

FIA   Future Internet Architecture

FIND   Future Internet Design

FIRE   Future Internet Research & Experimentation

FoS   Functionality of Service

FTP   File Transfer Protocol

FUNCOMP   Functional Composition

GAPI   A G-Lab Application-to-Network Interface

GENI   Global Environment for Network Innovations

GP   Goal Programming

GSM   Global System for Mobile Communications

G-lab   German Lab

HD   High Definition

HTML   HyperText Markup Language

IDP   Information Dispatch Point

IDT   Information Dispatch Table

IGMP   Internet Group Management Protocol

IEEE   Institute of Electrical and Electronics Engineers

IPDV   IP Packet Delay Variation

IPER   IP Packet Error Ratio

IPLR   IP Packet Loss Ratio

IPSec   IP Security

IPTD   IP Packet Transfer Delay

IPv4   Internet Protocol, version 4

IPv6   Internet Protocol, version 6

ISDN   Integrated Services Digital Network

ISO   International Organization of Standardization

ISP   Internet Service Provider

ITU-T   International Telecommunications Union - Telecommunication Standardization Sector

JBIG   Joint Bi-level Image Experts Group

JPEG   Joint Photographic Experts Group

LAN   Local Area Network

LZ   Lempel-Ziv

LZMA   Lemple-Ziv-Markov chain Algorithm

LZO   Lempel-Ziv-Oberhumer

LZW   Lempel-Ziv-Welch

lb   lower bound

MAC   Medium Access Control

MAUT   Multiple Attribute Utility Theory

MCDA   Multi-Criteria Decision Analysis

MCDM   Multi-Criteria Decision Making

MDCM   Multi-Domain Communication Model

MOP   Multi Objective Programming

MP   Micro-Protocol

MP3   MPEG-1 or MPEG-2 Audio Layer III

MPEG   Moving Picture Experts Group

MTU   Maximum Transfer Unit

NAC   Network Access Control

NAT   Network Address Translation

NENA   Netlet-based Node Architecture

NI   Network Interface

NIC   Network Interface Card

NML   Network Management Language

NSD   Network State Descriptor

OSI   Open System Interconnection

OSPF   Open Shortest Path First

OWL   Web Ontology Language

Panlab   Pan European Laboratory Infrastructure Implementation

PDU   Protocol Data Unit

PF   Packet Filter

PG   Protocol-Graph

PGF   Progressive Graphics File

PKI   Public Key Infrastructure

PLR   Packet Loss Ratio

QoE   Quality of Experience

QoS   Quality of Service

RAM   Random Access Memory

RARP   Reverse Address Resolution Protocol

RBA   Role-Based Architecture

RCI   Random Consistency Index

RDF   Resource Description Framework

RFC   Request for Comment

RINA   Recursive InterNetwork Architecture

RIP   Routing Information Protocol

RNA   Recursive Network Architecture

RND   Recursive Negotiation Descriptor

ROS   Remote Operation Service

RPC   Remote Procedure Call

RSH   Role-Specific Headers

RTP   Real-time Transport Protocol

RTSP   Real-time Streaming Protocol

RTT   Round Trip Time

SCS   Session Configuration Specification

SCTP   Stream Control Transmission Protocol

Self-Net   Self-Management if Cognitive Future Internet Elements

SIG   Special Interest Group

SILO   Services Integration, controL and Optimization

SIP   Session Initiation Protocol

SLS   MPEG-4 Scalable Lossless Coding

SMTP   Simple Mail Transfer Protocol

SMTP   Simple Mail Transfer Protocol

SOA   Service Oriented Architecture

SONATE   Service Oriented Network Architectures

SOP   Service Oriented Paradigm

SQL   Structured Query Language

SRDL   Service Request Description Language

S&C   Selection and Composition

TCP   Transmission Control Protocol

TCP/IP   Transmission Control Protocol / Internet Protocol

TKO   Transport Kernel Object

TMC   Transport Metric Configuration

TSA   Transport Service Adjustment

TSC   Transport Service Class

TTL   Time To Live

ub   upper bound

UDP   User Datagram Protocol

URI   Uniform Resource Identifier

VPN   Virtual Private Network

W3C   World Wide Web Consortium

WAN   Wide Area Network

WLAN   Wireless Local Area Network

WSDL   Web Services Description Language

WWW   World Wide Web

XIA   eXpressive Internetwork Architecture

XML   eXtensible Markup Language

1 Introduction

Driven by the need to share a limited number of large and powerful research computers, the Internet started its journey as the Advanced Research Projects Agency network (ARPANET) that carried its first packet on 1969 between the University of California, Los Angeles and the Stanford Research Institute. Through the time, the number of applications and the number of communication technologies have been evolved.

The number of Internet applications is increasing day-by-day. Some of them are telnet, email, World Wide Web (WWW), peer-to-peer (p2p), Skype, Flickr, Facebook and YouTube. Initial applications were telnet and email. Telnet is an application which provides access to a command line interface of a remote host and was developed in 1969. The first ARPANET email was sent in 1971. Tim Berners-Lee invented the world wide web in 1989 through which it was possible to use hypertext. Research and development on peer-to-peer technologies was started in the beginning of the 1990s. Skype is a voice over ip application which was exposed in 2003. Facebook is a social networking site which was launched in February 2004. In February 2005, YouTube came into the light. Each of these applications has its own requirement.

The number of communication technologies have also been increased. Initial technologies in the early 1970s were ARPANET, ALOHAnet and Ethernet. 2G (GSM) was commercially launched in Finland in 1991. At the end of 1990s, standards for wireless LAN were made. On 1st of October 2001, NTT DoCoMo launched the 3G technology (CDMA, CDMA 2000). Now-a-days, One of the 4G technologies such as LTE have already been deployed in many developed countries. Right now, researchers are working towards 5G technology. Each of this technology has its own capability. For example, The peak upload speeds of WIMAX, LTE and LTE advanced are 56 Mbit/s, 50 Mbit/s and 500 Mbit/s respectively.

Now the question is, what is the right glue to put between the applications and the communication technologies so that the requirements of the applications can be met. The answer was given by the networking community in 1970s and early 1980s by providing OSI model [144] and TCP/IP model [121][114]. Both of the models have several layers. Each layer offers services to the upper layer and the upper layer consumes those services. These models fulfill modularity (i.e., several layers) and abstraction (i.e., services provided by each layer) principles.

However, since applications with new requirements have emerged and the (virtual [91]) network technologies with new capabilities have been developed, network engineers could not retain the principles of the models and modified them according to their needs, which results in an architectural patchwork with many new protocols (i.e., IPv6, DCCP, ICMPv6), cross layer functionalities (i.e., QoS, Firewall, and Mobility services provided by several layers) and sub-layers (i.e., IPSec as layer 3.5, TLS as layer 4.5).

To solve those issues, several work have been done in the mid 1990s: Adaptive [103], DaCaPO [130] and FCSS [120]. Recently, for researching towards clean slate approaches and experimenting them in the real world scenario, several Future Internet Architecture (FIA) projects such as XIA [143], ChoiceNet, Named Data Networking, MobilityFirst, NEBULA have been funded by the National Science Foundation's (NSF) Future Internet Design (FIND) [40] and Network Science and Engineering (NetSE) program in the USA [84], G-Lab [46] by the federal ministry of education and research (BMBF) in Germany, Future Internet Engineering [38], 4WARD [6], ANA [9], IRATI [59], and AUTOI [11] by the European Commission, to name a few.

The results of some of these projects are a set of future network architectures such as Autonomic Network Architecture (ANA) [62], Netlet-based Node Architecture (NENA) [132], eXpressive Internetwork Architecture (XIA) [52], Forwarding on Gates [41], Service-Oriented Network Architectures (SONATE) [81], and Recursive InterNetwork Architecture (RINA) [98].

Some of these work such as ANA, NENA and SONATE have been done because it is hard to introduce new functionalities into the Internet and remove existing functionalities from the Internet because a lot of implicit dependencies exist between the protocols and the layers. For example, replacing IPv4 with IPv6 was not possible in the last 15 years. The addressing protocol IPv6 was standardized as IPv4 could not fulfill the addressing demands (i.e., the number of devices to be addressed) of the users. Moreover, as protocols are tightly coupled both horizontally and vertically, which results in difficulties in automatically switching between functionalities. Traditionally, an email application uses TCP, a Voice over IP (VoIP) application uses UDP, some video streaming applications use SCTP. However, a video application cannot just switch between UDP and SCTP based on its variety of demands. An example of vertical dependency was that for using IPv6, an update of TCP was required. According to RFC 2460 IPv6 Specification, "any

transport or other upper-layer protocol that includes the addresses from the
IP header in its checksum computation must be modified for use over IPv6,
to include the 128-bit IPv6 addresses instead of 32-bit IPv4 addresses" [31].
The problem is not limited to specific protocols or mechanisms. It is an
architectural issue.

For solving this architectural issues, SONATE has been proposed considering SOA design principles. SONATE is described in more detail in Section
2.

SONATE is based on communication services. A communication service
can represent a fine-grained functionality such as an algorithm for forward
error correction (e.g., hamming code) or compression (e.g., huffman tree)
or it can even represent a coarse-grained functionality such as the functionalities of the TCP/IP network stack or an access technology such as
WiFi.

A communication service can be offered by describing its capabilities
which are a set of effects provided by its implementation (i.e., a protocol or
a mechanism). For example, a retransmission service can be described by the
effects $DataLoss = 0\%$ and $LossDetection = true$. Similarly, a communication service can be requested by an application, in particular, an application
developer or a user by describing a set of effects which he is interested in.
For example, when an application requires the effects $DataLoss = 0\%$ and
$LossDetection = true$, a retransmission service might be selected and used.
For describing both application requirements and network offerings, a description language is required.

Most of the future network architectural approaches including SONATE
need to use a suitable service, or to select the best service, if there more than
one suitable service is available. Actually, two or more services offering the
same functionality with differing quality parameters might be provided by

the same service provider (using one specific architecture and different selection and composition approaches) or by different service providers (using
different architectures).

Selection of a suitable service can be done by matching the description
of the offered services with the description of the application requirements.
This match can result in several suitable services. Now, the question is,
which suitable service should be selected and used? The answer is that we
should select the best one, as we do in our day-to-day life.

Selecting the best service using a single selection criterion is trivial. For
example, if there are two communication services where one offers 100 ms
end-to-end delay and another offers 200 ms, then we should obviously select
the one with the lowest delay.

However, communication services have multiple selection criteria such
as delay, throughput, loss ratio, jitter and cost. Therefore, selecting the
best communication service is a Multi-Criteria Decision Making problem
(MCDM). For solving such a problem, several Multi-Criteria Decision Analysis (MCDA) approaches are used in managerial science such as Multiple Attribute Utility Theory (MAUT), Analytic Hierarchy Process (AHP),
ELECTREIII and Evamix [79].

AHP is used here to select the best service. The main requirement for
using AHP is to assign pairwise priority both for the requirements and for
the offers. However, as offerings are decoupled from the application requirements, mapping mechanisms are required to translate from the measured/es-
timated values of the offerings (which are described using the proposed description language) to priorities. In this thesis, two mapping mechanisms
have been proposed: round monotonic interpolation and fractional monotonic interpolation.

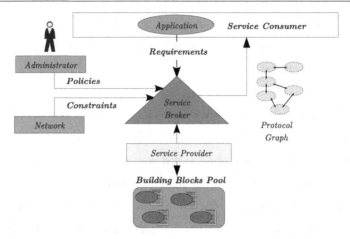

Fig. 1.1 A model for fine-grained service selection and composition [68]

The proposed work assists in "decoupling applications from the network stacks" which has several advantages. Firstly, both applications and networks can be developed and deployed independently and be used as soon as they are available. Secondly, it enables infrastructure provider to be separated from the application provider [37].

1.1 Problem Statement

The evolution of the Internet is slow because it is hard to introduce new functionalities or to update existing functionalities as its deployed functionalities are inherently tightly coupled with themselves and with the applications. So, a rethinking of network architectures is required [24]. For solving the problem, a service oriented network architecture (SONATE) has been proposed [81], as shown in Figure 1.1. In SONATE, the services provided by building blocks (BBs) are offered to the selection and composition engine

(S&C), which composes them based on the requirements, policies, and constraints to produce protocol graphs. Suitable protocol graphs, or the best protocol graph, are used for communication with other nodes in the network. SONATE, as a "Selection and Composition," [54] approach, has a set of challenges.

Some of the challenges in the selection and composition approach are building blocks description, application and administrator requirements description, identifying dependencies between building blocks and services, rating services, finding the appropriate granularity of services, defining a taxonomy/ontology for services, finding selection and composition methods, and handling the heterogeneity of services [110].

The dissertation focuses on two of the challenges: description and selection.

The description challenge is: How, and what, to define an extensible communication language such as a taxonomy so that all of the inputs and output of the selection (and composition) approach such as application requirements, building blocks, network constraints, administrator policies, services and protocol graphs can be described using the same language?

The selection challenge is: How to select the best service as soon as they are available?

1.2 Research Methodology and Scientific Contribution

The thesis contributes to two of the challenges: description and selection.

The challenges of defining taxonomy and describing building blocks, services, and application and administrator requirements are tackled by

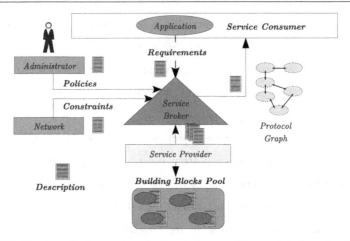

Fig. 1.2 The places in the service selection and composition model where descriptions are required [68]

proposing a communication service description language. The description language was first proposed in [68].

The selection challenge is tackled by adapting Analytic Hierarchy Process (AHP) with different mapping mechanisms which map the measured or estimated offerings of network services to their priorities. The mapping mechanism was first proposed in [66].

1.2.1 Service Description

Figure 1.2 and 1.3 show where description is needed in service oriented network architecture. My approach to tackle the description challenges was to analyze general selection (and composition) and some architectures that implement selection (and composition) including SONATE, Adaptive, DaCaPO, ANA, NENA, and FoG, and follow system design principles including

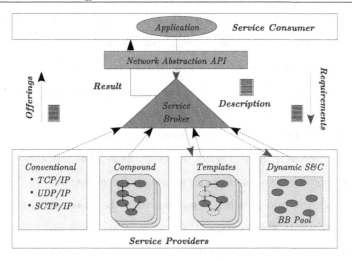

Fig. 1.3 The places in the selection model where descriptions are required [68]

modularity and abstraction, to derive the requirements for the description language. Based on the derived requirements, a communication service description language has been developed. The description language is shown to handle the description challenges in selection (and composition) approaches (see in Section 3.5).

1.2.2 Service Selection

Service selection is necessary during the selection (and composition) process and in the circumstances shown in Figure 1.3. My approach to tackle the selection challenges was to analyze those circumstances and find out their requirements. Moreover, a set of existing selection methods from the managerial science have been analyzed to find out which methods can be used to select communication services in service oriented network architectures.

An analytic hierarchy process (AHP) [100] has been adapted in this dissertation. As with all MCDA approaches, the adapted AHP can be used to select the best service from a set of suitable services (as determined by the application requirements). A process is proposed to filter the set of suitable services from the set of all possible services.

When more than one suitable services is available, the adapted analytic hierarchy process is used to select the best service. The adaptation of the analytic hierarchy process is made by using different mapping mechanisms to calculate the prioritization of services with the "measured/estimated" values provided by the offerings.

Composition methods such as netlets [131] as used in NENA and template based composition require selecting an appropriate netlet, a building block or a template during design time or runtime which can benefit from the work proposed in this dissertation.

1.2.3 Thesis Contributions

The contributions of the dissertation can be categorized into two main parts:

First, the communication service description language which is used to describe the requirements of the application, the offerings of the (building blocks and) protocol graphs, network properties, and administrator constraints. The description of the offerings of the building blocks assists in composing them to make a protocol graph based on the application requirements, network and administrator constraints. The description language is shown to handle the description challenges in selection (and composition) approaches.

The description of the application requirements helps in selecting building blocks for composition to constitute protocol graphs and in selecting the best protocol graph to use for the communication.

The second part of the dissertation proposes selection processes to select suitable services and the best service by using a matching process and an adapted analytic hierarchy process [100]. The adaptation of the analytic hierarchy process is accomplished by using mapping mechanisms.

1.3 Contributions Scope

The work, presented in this thesis, is done as a part of a project work where service oriented network architectures have been studied. As other colleagues also worked on different issues of the same architecture, the work are closely related and the results of one's work is complementary to others work.

1.3.1 Contributions Affiliated with the Project

The scientific contribution of this dissertation was accomplished as a part of the German-Lab (in short G-Lab) research project which was funded by the federal ministry of education and research in Germany [46]. The objective of the project was to develop clean-slate network architectures and communication mechanisms that are more evolvable and adaptive than today's Internet. In addition, the project was promised to provide an experimental facility where those architectures and mechanisms can be experimented.

Towards this goal, the project in the first phase had seven work packages as shown in Figure 1.4. The contribution of this thesis falls in the work

packages 1 (ASP 1) and 6 (ASP 6) are marked by red-colored ticks in the
Figure.

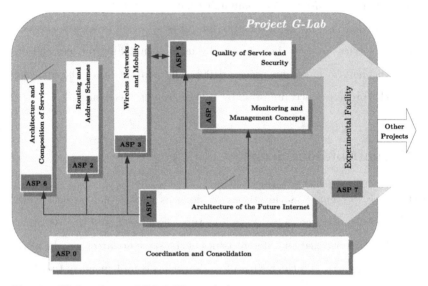

Fig. 1.4 Work packages of G-Lab Phase 1 [47]

1.3.2 Contributions to the SONATE Architecture

The current implementation components of the Service Oriented Network
Architecture (SONATE) are shown in Figure 1.5. The components work as
follows: 1, the application sends it requirements to the management controller through the network abstraction API, 2, the management controller
passes those requirements to the service broker, 3, the broker then forwards
those requirements to the templates and dynamic selection and composition engines to constitute protocol graphs, 4, the selection and composition

engines then use the repository of the building blocks where the implementation of the building blocks and their descriptions are stored, 5, the constructed protocol graphs are forwarded to the service broker, 6, the service broker then selects a suitable, or the best, protocol graph, 7, the management controller negotiates with the other nodes on the network so that they also use that particular protocol graph, 8, the application uses the selected protocol graph which is executed by the SONATE or other frameworks to communicate with the communication partner, 9, the connection termination is then handled by the management controller.

Currently, the implementation is used as an overlay on the top of the UDP/IP protocol. However, the concept can be applied to the lower layers.

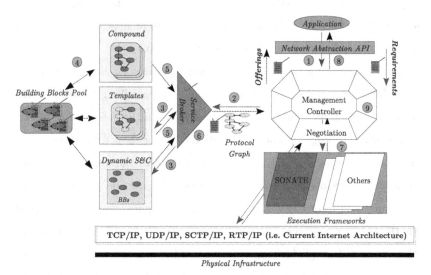

Fig. 1.5 Components of SONATE Implementation (adapted from [48])

The red-colored tick marks of the Figure 1.5 show the places where this thesis contributes to.

1.3.3 Relation with the Colleagues Work

The contribution of this thesis is closely related with the ongoing research work of my colleagues.

One of my colleagues proposed an efficient composition mechanism titled "Template-based Composition" [109] which requires the description of building blocks and the selection of a suitable, or the best, building block based on application requirements. This tasks can be assisted by the work presented in this thesis. Similarly, for selecting the best protocol graph, the selection mechanisms require the description of protocol graphs which can be produced by the "Template-based Composition" approach.

Another colleague sheds the lights on how to identify decision criteria for selecting different mechanisms which provide reliable transmission for service oriented network architectures [50]. For doing this, he analyzed retransmission and forward error correction mechanisms. His contributions are helpful for service description, especially, in describing building blocks so that selection mechanisms can get benefits from the described criteria.

The other colleague proposed evolutionary algorithms for runtime selection and composition [107]. The approach requires the description of application requirements and building blocks which can be provided by the work proposed in this thesis. Moreover, he is designing an efficient testbed for the networking research [106]. Towards this, he developed a Topology Management Tool (ToMaTo). By using ToMaTo, network researchers can design topology for experiments and can deploy in the real testbeds. Using ToMaTo, the network characteristics can be configured which requires description. The work presented in this thesis might benefit ToMaTo [49].

1.4 Outline of the Thesis

The outline of the dissertation is as follows. At first, the background of service oriented network architectures (SONATE), including the models where service description and service selection are necessary, is presented in Section 2.

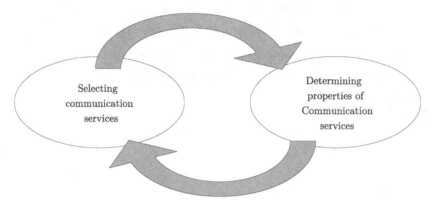

Fig. 1.6 Interdependencies between service selection and service description

The work of service description and service selection are complementary to each other as shown in Figure 1.6. For selecting communication services (i.e., service selection), it is necessary to determine and describe the capabilities of those services (i.e., service description). Chapter 3 describes service description. Service selection is discussed in Chapter 4.

Chapter 3 highlights on the proposed communication service description language which is required to describe the capabilities provided by communication services as well as application requirements, network, and other constraints. Moreover, description of communication services assists in selecting and composing building blocks and protocol graphs.

Chapter 4 presents the proposed service selection methods. Suitable, or the best, building block for composition and protocol graph for communication association, should be selected and used. Section 4.1 describes a matching process to select suitable services and Section 4.2 discusses an adapted analytic hierarchy process to select the best service. To select the best service automatically using process, a mapping mechanism is necessary to map from the measured value of the offers to the pairwise prioritization scale which is proposed in Section 4.2.2.5. The selection process is implemented and evaluated using a maximum of twenty two criteria and one hundred services which are discussed in Section 4.2.2.8.

Chapter 5 concludes the thesis.

2 Background: Service Oriented Network Architectures

Most of the issues in the Internet arise because of inflexibility and rigidness attributes of the network architecture, which is built upon a protocol stack. The problem that is faced by the Internet is that it is hard to integrate new functionalities in it and to remove existing functionalities from it. The reason is that protocols and layers are tightly coupled between themselves as well as within each other. In addition, they are also coupled with the applications. This problem is not limited to specific protocols and mechanisms. However, it is an architectural issue.

Similar problems were seen in software engineering which has evolved to manage complexities (e.g. maintenance, integration of new functionalities, time and task management) of development process, which has direct effects in terms such as of cost, quality and development time. That is why, for designing a new software architecture for the Internet core, the principles and techniques from software engineering can be applied.

Software engineering has evolved from structural programming to service oriented programming. The design of a future network architecture can benefit from software engineering techniques to make network architecture

more flexible and easy to maintain rather than having an ossified architecture (e.g. Internet).

The Service Oriented Network Architecture (SONATE) [82][97], a clean
slate network architecture, applies the principles of Service Oriented Architecture (SOA) to communication systems.

Services are the essential elements of a SOA. The protocol stack of the
Internet has also been developed considering services.

2.1 Layering in Protocol Stacks

To reduce complexity and promote modularity, the protocol stack has been
organized as layers. The International Organization for Standardization
(ISO) had specified seven layers for the Open System Interconnection (OSI)
model namely physical, data link, network, transport, session, presentation
and application [144]. The TCP/IP model has 5 layers as it integrates all of
the functionalities of the session, presentation and application layers of the
OSI model into one layer called application layer [113]. Each layer provides
services to its upper layer and consumes services from its lower layer.

An example scenario is shown in Figure 2.1 where a user started browsing
Internet using the WLAN connection of his laptop. In this case, the browser
sends the request to the server using Hyper Text Transfer Protocol (HTTP).
The packet is then sent to the TCP protocol of the transport layer which
encapsulates the HTTP packet and wraps its with its own header and trailer
around it. The transport layer then sends the packet to the IP protocol of
the network layer which does the same, i.e., encapsulates the TCP packet
coming from transport layer and adds its own header and trailer. The packet
is then sent to its lower layer so called link layer. The IEEE 802.11 protocol

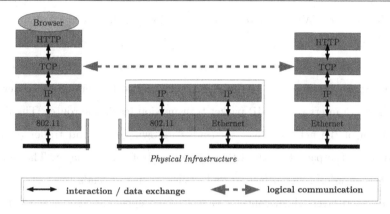

Fig. 2.1 Communication using layered network stacks (adapted from [121])

of the MAC layer does the same function and sends the packet to its physical layer which changes the bits into analog signals and transmits it.

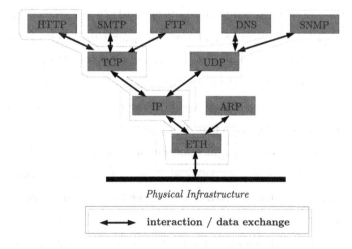

Fig. 2.2 Protocol graph in the current networks (adapted from [121])

The receiver (WLAN router) gets the analog signal, converts that into a sequence of bits and sends that to the IEEE 802.11 protocol of the MAC layer. The MAC layer extracts and modifies its header and trailer if necessary and sends the packet to the IP protocol (network layer) of the router. There is an internal IP-to-IP packet transmission inside the router. The IP protocol of the network layer then adds its own header and trailer to it and sends the packet to the Ethernet protocol of the link layer. The link layer then adds its own header and trailer to it and sends the packet to its physical layer which converts the bits into signals and sends it to the physical layer of the server. The physical layer of the server then changes the signals back into bits and sends the bits to the Ethernet protocol of the link layer. The link layer then extracts its headers and trailers and sends the IP packet to the network layer. Similarly, the IP protocol of the network layer extracts its header and trailer and sends the packet to the TCP protocol of the transmission layer. The TCP protocol of the transmission layer extracts its header and trailer and sends the packet to HTTP protocol of the application layer in the server side. The server receives the request and then sends its replies using the mentioned procedures. It is worthy to note that the router (i.e., the middle boxes) does not change the contents of the higher layers like TCP or HTTP packets.

A user usually has several applications running on his machine like browsing Internet and running a network management application. In that case, the set of protocols that are used in a sequence for all applications are not same. The sequence of protocols that are used to run an application is called a "Protocol graph". As shown in Figure 2.2, a browser uses the red marked protocol graph (HTTP-TCP-IP-ETH) and network management application uses green marked protocol graph (SNMP-UDP-IP-ETH).

As there are not many alternative protocols in the same layer, the number of protocol graphs used today is limited.

2.2 Service Oriented Architectures (SOA)

The three main entities of a basic service oriented architecture are service provider, service consumer and service broker [89] as shown in Figure 2.3. In the thesis, the color codes for service provider, service broker, and service consumer are chosen as pale green, blue, and light grey respectively. A service provider creates and registers its service to the service broker. A service consumer searches its required service to the service broker. After finding the service, he binds with the service for consuming.

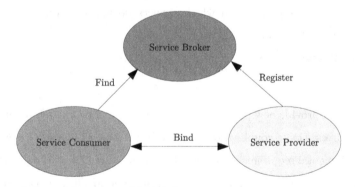

Fig. 2.3 Roles and Operations of SOA [89]

Eight main principles of SOA are as follows [35][36].

Loose coupling: Coupling refers to the degree of dependencies and bounding between two components. Loose coupling defines independence of a service; where in order to execute own functionalities a service does not require to have a knowledge about other services.

Service contract: A communication agreement which is covered by service description(s) or related documents.

Autonomy: Control of a service over the logic it encapsulates characterizes the autonomy.

Abstraction: Services are independent of the logic they use and those logic is hidden from the outside world.

Re-usability: A service should be independent and fine-grained enough so that it can be used later on with no or minor modification.

Composability: An ability of a service to be coordinated to other services for forming a composite service. Composability fosters re-usability of a service.

Statelessness: A property in which services do not keep the state after request has been processed.

Discoverability: A service should be descriptive enough to be discovered easily.

SOA can provide new prospects to build a future network architecture as SOA addresses loose coupling, re-usability and autonomy of a service, which are fundamental requirements of a flexible architecture. The OSI or TCP/IP protocol stack can be decomposed into various functionalities which are described with formal contract (i.e service description) as it makes functionalities autonomous and self-descriptive. A self-descriptive functionality has the ability to be discovered as it carries attached description which can be processed by the discovering entity. Abstraction is another point to be taken into account while decomposing a network stack (TCP/IP, UDP/IP, SCTP/IP) into various functionalities, it should be at the abstract level where it does not rely on a particular implementation thus logic should be hidden from the users and applications. Characteristics of a functionality such as autonomy, description and re-usability, make it composable. The concept of composability fosters ease of integration of functionalities. Nevertheless, the statelessness principle of SOA might not be appropriate for all functionalities of a network architecture as some functionalities of a network do require to keep the state (e.g. reliable transmission).

2.3 Service-Oriented Network Architectures (SONATE)

Now the question is: how to apply the SOA design principles on networks? Techniques like Web-Services and XML data structures were designed for the interplay of distributed autonomous functionalities on application level as shown in Figure 2.4a. Network functionalities like routing, data encoding, or flow control itself are inherently distributed as shown in Figure 2.4b. Thus specialized concepts for building networks according to SOA principles as well as new techniques for supporting SOA are required. The following subsection 2.3.1 provides an overview of such concepts.

2.3.1 Basic Concepts of a Service Oriented Network Architecture

Services are the main elements of a SOA. A service represents the effects of an activity rather than algorithms and data structures, i.e. a service represents a higher abstraction level since different algorithms may implement the same service. A building block is the implementation of an atomic com-

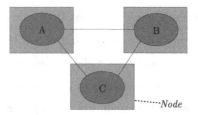

a) distributed autonomous services

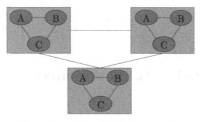

b) services of distributed functionality

Fig. 2.4 Network functionalities are inherently distributed in contrast to services on the application level [67]

munication service. A Micro-Protocol (MP) can be an example of a building block such as retransmission, data encryption (AES 256), and error correction (hamming code). Usually, each building block has several effects, for instance, reliable or confidential data transmission. But, there are also effects like increasing the end-to-end delay or reducing the maximum payload size. All the effects of a building block represent its services. The interfaces of a building block should reflect the provided services and hide the implementation details. Building blocks should also use generic interfaces so that the interaction between building blocks does not require extra adapters.

It is necessary that there are explicit service descriptions. Such descriptions should include effects and interfaces as shown in Figure 2.5. The effects of a service are offered through interfaces. The methods or operations that are exposed by web services are described using web service description

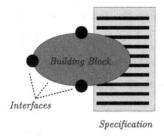

Fig. 2.5 Components of a building block description [67]

language (WSDL) along with the message format and protocol details. As a communication service is offered by a self-contained building block, the operations and message formats that are exposed by building blocks are hidden and only the resultant outcomes (i.e., effects) need to be described which necessitates a language to describe communication services. In this thesis, a communication service description language has been developed to fulfill this demand.

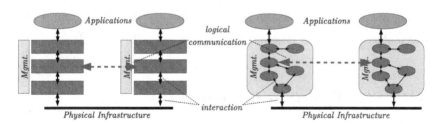

Fig. 2.6 Layerless network architecture [67]

Flexibilty can be achieved if we apply the SOA principles into the network. A network architecture should be flexible in two means. Firstly, networks should be able to adapt to specific customer or application needs and changing environmental conditions. Secondly, networks should be able to evolve, i.e. to add a new functionality, to change, update, or remove an existing functionality. This flexibility is achieved by composing several (smaller) services to a more complex and specialized service. In today's networks, complex protocols are organized in layers, building a static protocol graph [87]. Service oriented network architectures aim at supporting dynamic composition of services, i.e. dynamic protocol graphs as shown in Figure 2.6. Without being dependent on a static protocol graph, it is easier to make use of new protocols (i.e. building blocks) and to reuse functionalities on different levels. Having dynamic protocol graphs implies that there is no static placement of functionalities as defined by the layers of the OSI reference model. In this sense such networks will be layerless including compression/encryption can be used for application payload only or also for some protocol headers. Furthermore, it is not necessary that protocols are processed in sequence, for example, there might be different branches in the protocol graph to handle different but related data types within one flow, e.g. signalling and streaming media. In order to enable dynamic protocol graphs the interaction between building blocks should not be defined by executable code, but by description which can be easily changed.

2.3.2 SOA Principles in Networks

In order to fulfill the SOA principles, it is crucial to design services and building blocks appropriately. Nevertheless, the basic concepts of a service oriented network architecture described above support a service oriented design. Using service as the basic element for the design of a system instead of algorithms or protocols foster loose coupling and abstraction. Service descriptions represent the service contracts and are also used to discover services. Building blocks should be largely independent of its environment to achieve autonomy. Generic interfaces of building block make them composable. The layerless architecture implies higher probability for reusing of functionalities. Statelessness can not be achieved, in general, because some functionalities can be implemented only using state-full micro-protocols. In addition, there may be generic states, e.g. for the connection setup, the release phase, the states for failure, or the debug modes.

2.3.3 Service Composition

The purpose of service composition is to make a protocol graph by orchestrating services provided by several functionalities (building blocks). This is done by considering application requirements, network constraints and administrator settings. According to SOA principle, a service can represent any range of logic from any types of sources including other services. Thus, the resultant protocol graph also offers a (complex) service.

2.3.3.1 Related Work

In the early 1990s, a small group of network researchers concentrated on dynamic micro-protocol composition. They decomposed the functionalities of existing protocol stacks into a set of micro-protocols, and then composed those micro-protocols dynamically based on incoming requests from an application. Some of those works are Dynamic Configuration of Protocols (DaCaPo) [129] and Function Based Communication Subsystem (FCSS)[120]. Birgit Geppert et. al. [45] point to a drawback of the above approaches and ask for a generic description so that new deployments can be facilitated and implementation customization can be kept to a minimum.

M. Vogt et. al. [130] focused on networking protocols rather than the functionalities, services or roles provided by those protocols which were focused on by Robert Braden et. al. [25] and R. Dutta et. al. [32]. Two of those architectures are Role-Based Architecture (RBA) [25] and Network Service Architecture [44]. RBA is seen as an abstract approach to a non-layered architecture. RBA is organized in standardized building blocks, which are called roles. Each role has its own role ID which reflects its functionalities. In the initial concept only a limited number of roles were considered. There can be multiple roles on a single node and a role can also be abstractly distributed over multiple nodes. RBA decomposes the network stack and introduces Role-Specific Headers (RSH) that address specific functionalities at each node, therefore the packet header structure will no longer be a stack, but a heap of headers. This use of RSH is the main concept for role interaction and composition in RBA.

Sivakumar Ganapathy and Tilman Wolf proposed the first design for a network service architecture [44]. A service controller (for example, one for each autonomous system, organized in a hierarchy) manages a number of network service nodes and, upon connection request, sets up the service processing sequence and the data transfer between the service nodes for each flow. The request is then passed to the neighboring service controller along the path to the destination for further setting up the connection.

Some recently completed and ongoing projects are on selection and composition. Those projects are Autonomic Network Architecture (ANA) [9], NetServ [111], Net-Silo [32], 4WARD [6], Self-Net (Self-Management if Cognitive Future Internet Elements) [108] and The Recursive Network Architecture (RNA) [124]. Descriptions of some of the aforementioned projects have been summarized in the state-of-the-art paper [54].

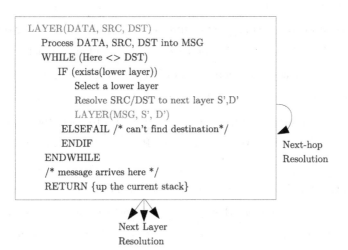

Fig. 2.7 Standard template for RNA metaprotocol [123]

A template-based approach is similar in concept to the NENA approach. In the NENA approach, netlets (i.e., a network stack) for each domain are composed during design time by network engineers assisted by software. Selection of an appropriate netlet is done during runtime by using MAUT[133]. However, the selection of appropriate mechanisms (i.e., building blocks) is not done in the NENA approach. In the template-based approach, not only appropriate templates are selected at runtime but also appropriate mechanisms are chosen.

Recursive Network Architecture (RNA), proposed by J. D. Touch et. al. [124], is a layer-based network architecture where each layer uses an instance of a unified and standard metaprotocol of the Multi-Domain Communication Model (MDCM)[140]. This reusable module, as shown in Figure 2.7, is used to provide basic functionalities which are necessary for each layer and every domain such as address resolution, alternative protocols/domains selection, and forwarding.

The concept was to compose metaprotocol stacks dynamically for different networking technologies like ethernet, wireless and optical networks by instanciating the common metaprotocol in different layers and configuring them. For composing network stacks, selection of the protocols should be done. However, they did not provide any mechanism to select the protocols. The proposed modified Analytic Hiearchy Process (AHP) can help in this regard.

However, MDCM uses a method to select the next domain. The method is to list and order them based on the distance from the source and select one which is the nearest in distance. However, this method is specific to select the next domain and cannot be used to select suitable or best protocols.

Role Based Architecture (RBA)[25] is a non-layered network architecture where network functionalities are decomposed into a set of smaller functionalities like encryption, decryption, compression, decompression, fragmentation, and reassembly. These functionalities are called roles reside in network nodes (routers, switches, workstations) and processes the packet. Similar to the current layered network architecture, each packet in RBA consists of a header and a payload. However, the header is organized as a heap rather than as a stack, thereby, the network functionalities can be provided in a random order as well. In RBA, the header contains a heap of Role Specific Header (RSH) which consists of role address and RSH body.

$$RSH(< RoleAddr >, ...; < RSHbody >)$$

A role in a node is addressed by the id of that role plus the node id or a wild card mask of node ids.

$$< RoleAddr >::=< RoleID > @ < NodeID > \mid < RoleID > @*$$

For example, the forwarding role instance of every router can be addressed as

$$RSH(HBHforward@*; dest - NodeID, src - NodeID)$$

In RBA, two roles can be composed into a larger role if those roles directly communicate with each other using RSHs and the inter-role data communication is replaced by shared data communication. Similarly, a coarse-grained role can be decomposed into fine-grained roles by providing their data communication facility using RSHs.

RBA requires each role to be specified. A suitable or the best roles should be selected if more roles with similar functionalities are available. However, they did not proceed on those topics. The proposed work of service description and selection can certainly help in the process of RBA.

The x-Kernel, an operating system kernel as well as an architecture for implementing network protocols, was proposed by Norman C. Hutchinson et. al. [58][57][88]. The basic idea behind x-Kernel is to decompose the monolithic module of networking protocols into a set of protocol modules and then to compose them at three different times by using a uniform protocol interface: configuration time, booting time and runtime. Protocol objects are composed statically at kernel configuration time. At kernel booting time, each protocol object runs some initialization code and calls the *open_enable* method of the lower level protocol from which it wants to receive messages (i.e, the protocol upon which it depends). For example, the higher level protocols TCP and UDP calls the *open_enable* of the lower level protocol IP and IP calls the *open_enable* operation of Ethernet. At runtime, an application program calls the *open* method of some protocol object to create a session. For instance, an application can call either TCP or UDP protocols for creating a new session.

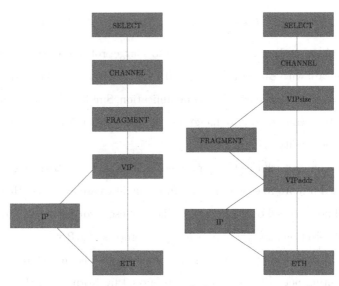

Fig. 2.8 Different configuration of RPC layers [58]

They mentioned the advantages of protocol decomposition as: firstly, each individual component is easier to implement, test, debug and optimize over monolithic module, secondly, existing protocol modules can be reused. They compared monolithic RPC with the layered RPC (i.e., decomposed the modules and then composed) and showed that the layered RPC has 0.14 ms more latency over monolithic RPC.

For composing protocols, selection of an appropriate protocol from a set of alternative protocols of the lower layer is done by a higher layer protocol at runtime. During configuration time, RPC layers can be configured in different ways as shown in Figure 2.8. The SELECT layer maps an RPC address (procedure ids) onto procedure addresses (server processes). The CHANNEL layer supports request/reply transactions. The higher level protocol creates a session by opening a channel such that it can receive a message through that channel. The FRAGMENT layer which is persistent, provides unreliable delivery of messages. The data can be lost on the way to the destination as well as it might arrive at the destination with different order as the message was sent. The protocol here is persistent meaning that the layer saves a copy of the data before transmitting so that the lost packet can be sent again. Hence, the FRAGMENT layer of the left figure does a sequence of tasks: 1, it fragments the packet if the size of the packet is more than 64k-bytes, 2, it adds sequence numbers onto the packet, 3, it sends the packet to the lower layer VIP. In this case, every packet goes through the FRAGMENT layer which has a cost of 0.21 ms of latency [58]. To reduce this cost, a VIPsize layer is added on the top of the FRAGMENT layer which checks the size of the message (Figure 2.8 right). For small packets, the VIPsize layer forwards the packet to the VIPaddr, otherwise, it forwards the packet to the FRAGMENT layer. This way, for the small packets, it is possible to save the cost of 0.15 ms of latency as 0.06 ms of latency is requred for checking the size of the packet in the VIPsize layer. The layer VIPaddr again checks the size of the packet. If the size of the packet is less than or equal to 1500 bytes then VIPsize selects ETH, otherwise it selects IP.

The selection process/policy of x-Kernel is very simple and is integrated in the higher layer protocol where the decision is taken. For example, VIPsize and VIPaddr take the decision (Figure 2.8 right). Changing of the selection policy requires to update the layer which is not possible when the policy is widely deployed. This tight coupling might hinder the evolution of the protocols.

The proposed work of service description (describing the policies in a generic way irrespective of the layers and protocols) and service selection (selection considering the policies) can help to solve the tight coupling problem of x-Kernel and in turn it can provide flexibility.

Christian Tschudin discussed disadvantages of OSI and TCP/IP approaches and proposed to provide a framework called "protocol stack environment" to compose a set of network functionalities like Remote Operation Service (ROS), Internet Protocol (IP), Address Resolution Protocol (ARP), Basic Encoding Rules (BER), and ISO Ethernet type LAN (8802) for making a customized stack based on application requirements [125]. Moreover, he proposed to download and install necessary functionalities at runtime. The framework contains a set of static entities of functionalities from where a set of instances can be created. These instances can either be anchored or free. A free or independent instance is usable only when that is anchored or connected with other instances. Two free instances can be anchored if their offered and required semantics matches. An anchored entity like ISO 8802 gives an immediate access to the communication service. He devised a so called 'toy environment' using PascalCom language for experimenting the concept like adding a new layer in the running protocol stack, replacing a running layer from the stack, distributing protocol stack on several environments at runtime and downloading functionalities for the bootstrap of a protocol stack. One purpose he mentioned of developing such a environment was to understand the management of running protocol stacks. Though he provided a mechanism to connect two layers just by semantics matching, however, he did neither provide concepts of how those instances can be described so that matching can be performed, nor he provided a mechanism for selecting a suitable or the best functionality when more functionalities are available.

Nina T. Bhatti et. al. [17] proposed a system for constructing high-level protocols which was based on the x-Kernel (discussed above) and provide more flexibility than x-Kernel. High levels protocols are those which offer rich functionalities like delivery of messages in a correct order to a set of processes. This approach provides a framework for composing and running micro-protocols (finer-grained than the x-Kernel protocols). The composed microprotocols can then again be composed with the external x-Kernel protocols to create a complete subsystem. The framework and external x-Kernel protocols communicate with each other by using the x-Kernel interface. In x-Kernel, protocols are composed hierarchically where a thread shepherds each message (one-thread-per-message) to a particular direction (from a upper layer protocol to a lower layer protocol) and no communication is possible between the protocols in the same layer. Bhatti's approach which is an event based (message arrival, timeout) supports mutiple-threads-per-message which assists in parallel execution of micro-protocols in the same layer.

In the Internet, a user has no control over packet handling, especially, packet forwarding decision. To provide such controls, Christian Tschudin et. al. [126] proposed to use network pointers below the IP layer, which are a a set of composable packet processing functions. Each network pointer is identified by an address. The functionalities that network pointers can provide are packet forwarding, header modification, multiplexing and demutiplexing, mapping to or from IP. Other functionalities can also be built in the pointer space.

Here the composition of network pointers is done statically. Using network pointers, a mobile personal area network can be constructed where a set of mobile devices can be connected to a cellular access point which is again connected to a fixed network. In this scenario, a pointer can be configured statically which forwards the packet from the fixed network to the cellular access point and the cellular access point can be configured to forward packets to the PDA, MP3 player and heart monitor. As in this case, the communication is done mostly in the data link layer, IP overhead is reduced.

However, in this approach, the selection of the network pointers is static which is tightly coupled.

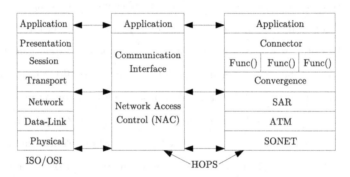

Fig. 2.9 Horizontally Oriented Protocol Structure (HOPS) [51]

Even though Zygmunt Haas proposed a protocol structure for high speed communication over broadband ISDN, the idea is technology agnostic [51]. In this approach, for decreasing delay and increasing throughput, the ISO/OSI layer is decomposed into three layers: application (A), communication interface (CI) and network access control (NAC). The NAC layer is hardware-based and the A layer is software-based. The CI layer acts as an interface between software and hardware and is a mixture of them. In the CI layer, functionalities of the higher layers (Transport to Presentation layer of the OSI model) are decomposed into a set of independent functions. Whereas layers are organized in horizontal manner, these independent functions are organized vertically so that they can run in parallel as shown in Figure 2.9. Examples of these functions are Retransmission, Connection-Option, Sequencing, Flow Control, Addressing, Presentation, Session Management, and Congestion Control. Although each function is considered to be independent, this is not usually the case. For example, Re-sequencing of packets is done when there is no error. This type of dependency is handled by the connector. The functions in CI gets raw information from NAC. Before passing it to the application layer, evaluation in terms of dependencies of these functions is done by the connector.

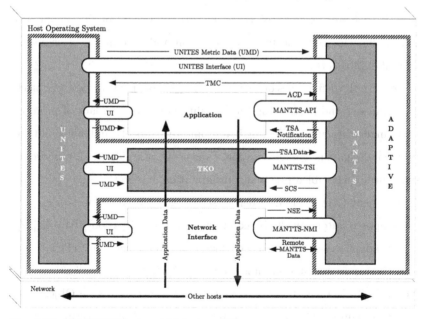

Fig. 2.10 ADAPTIVE System Architecture [22]

For selecting appropriate functions which is done by the Network Interface (NI), they suggested to use an individual selection algorithm which fits best for the user as selection requires policies which might be different for different users, environment, time and space. For example, in case of retransmission, selective retransmission mechanism can be chosen when average bit error rate (BER) is large. However, in case of reliable environment, go-back-n can be used. NI might also use its previous knowledge and experience for taking new decision or change its previous decision.

As functions are run in parallel, this approach can certainly improve performance if it can select suitable functions or the best function. For example, if it can select a function whose packet processing time is faster than alternatives, the resultant end-to-end delay can be reduced. However, they did not provide any protocol or algorithm for selection. This approach can get benefit from the proposed selection and description mechanisms presented in this thesis.

To solve the deficiencies of conventional transport network protocols such as extraneous and obstructing functionalities of protocols, lack of protocol performance because of selecting inappropriate protocols, and inflexibility of protocol design and implementation, Douglas C. Schmidt et. al. proposed a dynamically assembled protocol transformation, integration and evaluation environment (ADAPTIVE) where a set of reusable "building blocks" can be composed automatically based on functional specification [104][102][22].

The adaptive system consists of three main components: UNITES (UNIform Transport Evaluation Subsystem), MANTTS (Map Applications and Networks To Transport Systems) and TKO (Transport Kernel Objects) as shown in Figure 2.10. UNITES is responsible for selecting, collecting, analyzing and presenting metric, monitoring traffic and measuring performances of protocol. All of the collected data from UNITES help MANTTS to select

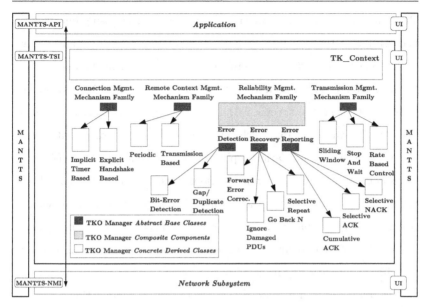

Fig. 2.11 Transport Kernel Objects (TKO) context [22]

policies and mechanisms and help TKOs to select and instantiate reusable mechanisms into executable session objects. TKO configures and composes the selected mechanisms into executable session objects as shown in Figure 2.11.

Even though adaptive systems can adapt by switching between the mechanisms based on the performance of applications and networks which they can precisely measure for a session, however, this approach concentrates only on multimedia applications.

Ariane Keller et. al. proposed a system architecture for evolving protocol stacks [62]. The proposed network architecture, an Autonomic Network Architecture (ANA) [9], is based on the principle of so called "indirection". In their architecture, the interaction between the FBs (which is similar to

BBs) within one node or between nodes is accomplished using information dispatch point (IDP's) which enables the decoupling of sending and receiving of functionalities. Binding between IDPs are stored in the information dispatch table (IDT). Public (can receive data from any FB) and private (receive data from the specific FB) IDPs have been introduced to control access of the available FBs, which can ensure certain level of security. They also proposed a communication application programming interface (API) to access node-local or network-wide functionalities. The main objective of this API is to enable flexibility without imposing restrictions on the implementation of any functionality. The authors claimed that runtime selection and composition of functionalities are possible using their approach, however, they did not propose any mechanism until now.

G. Canfora et. al. proposed a QoS-aware service composition based on Genetic Algorithm [27]. In this approach, an abstract service is constructed by selecting and composing a set of concrete services which meet the specified constraints and optimized according to the fitness criterion on QoS parameters. The advantages of this approach over linear programming are that, 1, it supports non-linear aggregation functions, 2, it scales with increasing the number of concrete services, and 3, the fitness function can be adapted, if necessary. However, as service composition is a np-hard problem, this approach might not be appropriate for runtime composition.

In the Services Integration, controL and Optimization (SILO) architecture which is proposed by R. Dutta. et. al., fine-grained composable services called silos which reside between the application and the network interface are composed dynamically in a per-flow basis [33]. They implemented and released a software prototype of their architecture [13]. However, they defined the dependencies between the services in a hard-coded way, which reduces flexibility.

Composition of communication services is a newer field compared to the composition of web services. Several approaches exist to do web service composition like Business Process Execution Languages (BPEL), Semantic Web (OWL-S), Web Components, Algebraic Process Composition, Petri Nets, Model Checking and Finite State Machines. Nikola Milanovic et. al. [78] compared all of these methods based on five requirements such as service connectivity, nonfunctional properties, composition correctness, automatic composition and composition scalability and showed that neither of these methods support all of these requirements.

2.3.4 Service Description

Service descriptions are used to specify several kinds of services. Firstly, the service offered by building blocks must be described. Secondly, descriptions of composed service are required. In case services are composed dynamically also the corresponding service description must be generated. Finally, applications use service descriptions (more specifically, a requirement description) for requesting a communication service. These service descriptions are then used by the service broker and by the selection and composition process. The service broker, being used at runtime of an application, requires that service descriptions are machine processable.

All kinds of service descriptions should use a common language to avoid language translations in the service broker or in the selection and composition process. Such a common description language must be comprehensive enough to describe all of the existing communication services. Moreover, the language must be extensible to describe future yet unknown services. It is likely to achieve this comprehensiveness and flexibility by using an RDF

(Resource Description Framework) like syntax or defining sets of properties with (simple) attributes only. It is important that the language can be extended without the need of modifying the service broker or the selection and composition mechanism so that both the language can be backward-compatible and scalable.

The service description language must enable distinction between mandatory and optional requirements from the point of view of an application and also to distinguish guaranteed and not guaranteed properties of an offered service. The reason is that it must be decidable if a service is appropriate, i.e. fulfills all mandatory requirements. Furthermore, non-mandatory aspects of a service can be used to find the optimal service.

Even though services should be designed and implemented so that they are autonomous, feature interaction among services is still possible. As an example, compression (i.e. compacting the payload or header) service and encryption (i.e. confidentiality) service where the processing sequence is not arbitrary as compression after encryption is not appropriate. If such interactions of feature between services or classes of services are known these may be described in policy rules. The problem is to ensure that all feature interactions are known, especially if new features are introduced.

2.3.5 Service Selection

It is likely that flexible networks will offer several similar communication services to applications which might be implemented with different protocols. In such a scenario, applications must not be aware of the utilized protocols. To achieve this, applications must only be aware of the provided service while the service implementation remains transparent for applica-

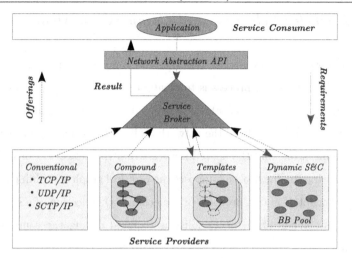

Fig. 2.12 A model for coarse-grained service selection in a service-oriented network architecture [68]

tions. This can be achieved by introducing a service broker which selects an appropriate service implementation at runtime (see Figure 2.12). A service is appropriate if it fulfills all mandatory application requirements. In addition services may differ regarding optional requirements which are used to determine the optimal service. A service broker might consider services provided by different sources. There may be standard protocol stacks, pre-composed services as well as dynamically composed services. This way a service broker also enables the simultaneous use of concurrent selection and composition approaches.

2.3.6 Service Selection and Composition Model

A model for fine-grained service selection and composition is shown in Figure 1.1. The aim of the process is to create a protocol graph for a network connection. To achieve this goal, the broker takes the requirements from the application, constraints from the network, policies from the network or system administrator, and the offered services from the network. Considering all of these inputs, the broker composes the protocol graph of building blocks (the implementation of a protocol or a mechanism). Selection of a suitable, or the best, fine-grained functionality is required during the composition process.

A model for coarse-grained service selection is shown in Figure 2.12. As with SOA, the three main entities in this model are the service consumer, the service provider, and the service broker. The service broker selects a suitable, or the best service, from the services offered by the different service providers by considering the requirements specified by an application developer through an application programming interface (API). Service providers can be categorized based on their composition approaches. Services can be offered by conventional providers like TCP/IP, UDP/IP, and SCTP/IP. Services can be composed during design time, deployment time, partial runtime and runtime. In compound approaches, services are composed during design time, potentially assisted by software. In this approach, the selection of an appropriate compound service is done during runtime. The template approach is an example of partial runtime composition, where the placement of functionalities is done during design time and a suitable, or the best, mechanism is chosen during runtime. Services can also be provided by a dynamic selection and composition provider where the selection and composition of the protocol graph is done during runtime.

Partial runtime and dynamic selection and composition providers cannot register their services to the broker until they get the application's requirements and perform their composition. Other providers can register their service to the broker beforehand.

Approaches for selection and composition face a trade-off between "Composition time" and "Information availability". Composition can be done at design, deployment and runtime. At design time, there are no time limitations for the composition process. Moreover, the requirements of application(s) (or application classes) are already known. At deployment time (i.e. when an application is deployed on a platform), long running calculations are not suitable. But, at this time, constraints of the platform, such as, the available access networks and general resource limitations are known. At runtime, there are hard time constraints for selection and composition, but only at this time specific user requirements (e.g. limits for costs) and dynamic network constraints (e.g. current network load) might be available. Examples for selection and composition approaches are: a) design time composition accomplished by humans possibly supported by tools; b) usage of templates, where the basic composition and especially the placement of functionalities are defined at design time and building blocks are selected to fill out place holders; c) selection and composition of coarse-grained building blocks, which have been pre-composed at an earlier time. As Figure 2.12 illustrates, different selection and composition approach may be performed at different points in time. No single composition approach is optimal in all cases.

The service broker returns a suitable, or the best, service to the application through the API.

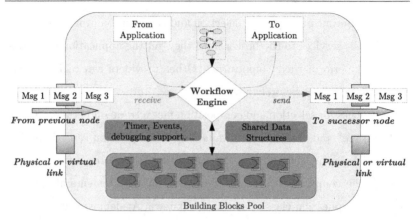

Fig. 2.13 SONATE framework [43]

2.3.7 SONATE Framework

After the protocol graph is chosen by the broker, it is sent to the SONATE framework for processing. The workflow engine of the SONATE framework executes that protocol graph. The components of the SONATE framework inside a node is shown in Figure 2.13. The workflow engine accepts the protocol graph description as an input and executes the building blocks in the sequences as described in the protocol graph. The workflow engine receives the application data from the same node or from the previous node. After processing the data, it sends the data either to its own application or to the next node for processing.

The framework is available in every intermediate and end nodes on the network.

2.3.8 Signaling of Protocol Graphs

After choosing the protocol graph, the resultant description of the protocol graph is sent to the other communication endpoint so that the communication partner also uses the same protocol graph for communication. This process is called protocol graphs signaling 2.14. The mechanisms for protocol graph signaling is independent of selection and composition algorithms.

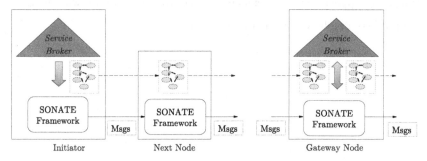

Fig. 2.14 Signalling of Protocol Graphs [43]

The intermediate nodes may act as firewalls or gateways by altering the protocol graphs. They might also request different behavior from the sender by providing feedback.

2.4 Summary

Applying SOA principles in network architectures can make them flexible in both long-term and short-term.

The long-term flexibility can be achieved by exchanging building blocks and protocol graphs. Building blocks are self-contained and have well defined interfaces and their interactions are exposed only by descriptions which are easier to exchange than the exchange of today's layer. As protocol graphs are also exposed by their descriptions, they can easily be exchanged than today's exchange of network stacks.

The short-term flexibility can be achieved by using selection and composition algorithms which generates description of protocol graphs based on the application requirements, network constraints, and administrator settings. When the application requirements and network constraints will change, the protocol graphs will be adapted itself as well.

3 Service Description

A communication service (in short, a service), a set of effects provided by an execution of an implementation of protocol(s) or mechanism(s), is described by its "Service Description". Existing web service description languages such as WSDL [139], which are used to describe web services, are not suitable for describing communication services as these two types of services differ in their basic characteristics. The methods or operations that are exposed by web services are described using WSDL along with the message format and protocol details. Considering a flexible architecture such as SONATE, a communication service is offered by a self-contained building block, the operations and message formats that are exposed by building blocks are hidden and only the resultant outcomes need to be described which necessitates a language to describe communication services.

Such a language must not be specific to any composition method so that they are scalable and extensible. Moreover, all of the components of a selection (and composition) method should speak a common language so that no intermediate translation is required [96]. The requirements for the language is described in Section 3.2. To tackle the challenges, a communication service description language is proposed in Section 3.3. Before that, the related work of service description is discussed in Section 3.1. Section 3.4 describes how the proposed language fulfills the requirements. The chapter is concluded with the validation of the language.

3.1 Related Work

L. Völker and D. Martin et. al. [133] provided a model to determine the composite properties of a netlet which can been seen as an ordered set of pre-composed functional blocks according to their order of execution that constitute a protocol stack. The properties after the functional block i, ρ_i depend on the properties of data coming from the previous functional block, ρ_{i-1}, the effects of the functional block i, Ψ_i, on the properties ρ_{i-1} and the global state of the nodes and its interfaces Ξ which can be expressed as

$$\rho_i = f(\rho_{i-1}, \Psi_i, \Xi) \tag{3.1}$$

The total effects of a netlet on the properties can be expressed as

$$\rho_n = f(f(...(f(\rho_0, \Psi_1, \Xi), ...), \Psi_{n-1}, \Xi), \Psi_n, \Xi) \tag{3.2}$$

Considering processing delay, the required time of a functional block to process a packet which is added in every functional block as the packet passes through it. The hardware which executes the functional block has an effect on the processing delay. Processing delay decreases as the capabilities of the hardware increases. Processing delay is also dependent on the global state such as the current CPU cycle.

Their model on aggregating properties is simple. However, they did neither mention which type of effects can a functional block have on the properties such as addition, subtraction, multiplication or division nor did they provide any model to describe them.

Bernd Reuther et. al. [96][97] provided a model for service oriented communication systems and specified both the requirements of the service user and the offerings from the service provider using two types of properties: inherent and qualitative. They specified each communication service CS_i as a set of those properties.

$$CS_i = \{Pi_i, Pq_i\} \ where \ Pi_i = \{pi_1, ..., pi_n\} \ and Pq_i = \{pq_1, ..., pq_n\} \quad (3.3)$$

If specified as requirements, the first one expresses necessary properties and is used to select suitable services from the offered services, the second one expresses desired properties and is used to select the most suitable one among the suitable services. How this specification assists in selecting suitable services and the best service is discussed in the related works of the Sections 4.1.1 and 4.2.1.

They specified each inherent property, Pi_i as

$$Pi_i = (URI, \ lb, \ ub) \quad (3.4)$$

where each inherent property Pi_i is identified by a unique URI, lb and ub determine the lower bound and upper bound of that property. The semantics to specify the inherent properties of the offerings are

$$\forall x \in [lb^O, \ ub^O] \quad (3.5)$$

For example, an inherent property, MTU, for the offerings can be expressed as (http://www.icsy.de/ inherent/properties/MTU, 0, 1400). This means that the maximum transfer unit is between 0 and 1400 bytes.

The semantics to specify the inherent properties of the requirements are

$$\exists x \in [lb^R, ub^R] \tag{3.6}$$

For example, an application requirement for MTU can be expressed as (http://www. icsy.de/inherent/properties/MTU, 500, 1200). That means, the application requires to send packets in size between 500 and 1200 bytes.

Qualitative properties, Pq_i, are not guaranteed and used to rate a service and are specified by

$$pq_i = \{URI, q, lb, ub, a, b, y\}$$
$$where \quad q \in [0,1] \wedge lb, ub, \in \Re \wedge y \in \Re^+ \wedge a, b \in [0,1] \tag{3.7}$$

where 0 indicates "worst" quality and 1 indicates the "best" quality. For example, a qualitative property "delay" can be specified as a requirement as $pq_i = \{http://www.icsy.de/qualitative/properties/delay, f(50) = 0.5, 200, 10, 0, 0, y\}$. This means that the application can work well from 10 ms to 200 ms delay but 50 ms should be considered as a medium quality.

Quality of the offered services can be specified in two ways: i, subjective method, and ii, objective method. In the subjective method, the quality is determined by the experts while for the objective method, the quality is determined based on benchmarks.

This quality specification, based on non-linear rating functions which requires only one point to be specified (a, b), is specific to the approach and cannot be used in other mechanisms where more points are specified.

Micro-protocols, whose schema is shown in Figure 3.1, are the basic building blocks of configurable high level protocols [17]. They can have three types of events: exported, imported, and private. Exported events are exposed to other micro-protocols. Imported events are generated in other micro-protocols and handled by the micro-protocols which import that. Private events are used only for internal communication of a micro-protocol by declaring private data which are visible to all of the defined handlers of the micro-protocol.

micro-protocol *name* {
    ... *Decl of exported events, message attributes,*
        data inspection, modification routines ...
    ... *Decl of imported events, global variables* ...
    ... *Decl of private events, message, attributes, variables* ...
    ... *Initialization code* ...
    ... *Event handlers* ...
    ... *Data inspection routines* ...
    ... *Local procedures* ...
} end micro-protocol *name*

Fig. 3.1 Micro-protocol schema [17]

When a micro-protocol would like to expose certain functionalities to other micro-protocols, it can do so by exporting data inspection and modification routines.

In this scheme, dependencies between micro-protocols are hard-coded by using import and export of events and data inspection and modification routines. Any addition, deletion and modification of import and export policies requires to change the code inside the micro-protocol. Moreover, micro-protocol developers must be aware of other available events and routines which might not be feasible at all.

Donald F. Box et. al. [104][102][22] proposed a specification scheme for their proposed adaptive system as existing specification schemes [145][95][29] are neither flexible nor adaptive to changing application requirements and network characteristics. As the name indicates, the proposed "adaptive system" composes and adapts later on, if necessary, flexible and reusable building blocks to make customized protocol graph for each session. Several components called "ADAPTIVE communication descriptors (ACD)" are employed to specify those application requirements and network characteristics. These components are: Quality of Service (QoS), Functionality of Service (FoS), Data Synchronization and Delivery (DSD), Transport Service Adjustment (TSA), and Transport Metric Configuration (TMC).

	minimum acceptable	expected maximum	expected mean	expected variance
throughput	dont care	x	x	x
connection duration	x	maximum allowed	x	x
delay	x	x	unknown	x
jitter	x	x	x	x
loss probability	x	x	x	x

Table 3.1 Specification of application requirements using QoS parameters

Applications specify the qualitative description of a desired service using QoS. It specifies a set of qualitative parameters (e.x., throughput, delay, jitter) and a range of values for each parameter (e.x., minimum acceptable, expected mean) as shown in Table 3.1. Moreover, default values can be specified for each attribute of QoS parameters such as expected mean delay is unknown.

On the other hand, functional behaviors of a desired service are specified by the component "FoS". It specifies policies of what processing must be done before data transmission and reception. For example, encryption, recover from loss data.

Policies regarding organizing multiple data streams in a session is defined in DSD. For example, specifying the action to be taken in case of a stream synchronization failure. The policies of using mechanisms (such as read-/write call or in-kernel direct routing) to deliver the data to an application are also defined.

TSA facilitates applications to participate directly in the dynamic configuration of a communication session. TSA contains a set of statements with the construct <*condition, action*> where the *condition* specifies the events applications are interested in and the *action* specifies the tasks to be done in case of occurring the event. For example, when delay is more than 300 ms, please abort the connection.

Applications can specify performance metrics in TMC such as what performance parameters should be measured (throughput), where to be measured (end system), how often to be measured (every k ms) and what to do after the measurement (e.x., call back to the application or store in a repository).

Moreover, the adaptive system contains *Transport Service Class (TSC)* where a set of parameters are pre-specified for different transport service classes, *Remote Negotiation Descriptor (RND)* which stores negotiated parameters, *Network State Descriptor (NSD)* stores dynamic network properties and *Session Configuration Specification (SCS)* is the final specification of a session. Based on this configuration, the required building blocks are selected and composed.

Applications configure ACD through Application Programming Interface (API). The configuration is then sent to the TCS where an appropriate service class is chosen based on the configuration of ACD, RND, and NSD which is then sent to the SCS. Sometimes, ACD bypasses all of the intermediate steps and sends the settings directly to the SCS. In that case, SCS takes the configuration from NSDs and finalizes the session configuration.

Using the proposed communication service description language, both Quality of Service (QoS) and Quality of Experience (QoE) parameters can be expressed using the same construct. However, describing one of them might be enough as they are related to each other as shown by [39]. Thus, one type of parameter can be calculated and used when we know other types of parameter. Their mapping can be done during design time or run time automatically.

S. Unnikrishnan et. al. proposed a network management language (NML) which facilitates an application programmer to build network management applications using their query language [141]. NML is an extension over SQL, which provides the same functionalities as that of SQL language using a different syntax. The Data Manipulation Language (DML) is extended to include a network management specific concept of time/version. As the language was constructed to manage network resources, however, the language is not suitable to describe the capabilities of communication services.

For searching and selecting service offers, C. Popien et. al. provided a service request description language (SRDL) for distributed systems [92] where the syntax of the service request is

```
service-request ::= <service_request_operation>
<search-constraint> "END SERVREQ"
service_request_operation ::= <search_operation>
            |<select_operation>
```

```
search-operation ::= "SEARCH" <service-type-identifier> "WITH"
<conditionalmatching-criteria>
select-operation ::= "SELECT" <service-type-identifier> "WITH"
<conditionalselection-criteria>
```

An example of such a request is given below

```
SEARCH PRINTER WITH
IF SUCCESS location == CompCent AND
cost_per_page $ 0.10
THEN TAKE THAT
ELSE IF SUCCESS cost_per_page < 0.10 AND queue_length/d $ 3
THEN cost_per_page < 0.10 AND queue_length/d $ 5
ELSE location = CompCent END END
```

Though the language enables the specification of the matching criteria, selection criteria, search constraints, and policies, however, it does not consider the property values of the service offers as it is difficult to find the general description for such properties corresponding to all exporters (i.e., service providers).

Service description languages are not new to the web service community. The Web Services Description Language (WSDL) which is based on eXtended Markup Language (XML) has been standardized by the World Wide Web Consortium (W3C) in 2007 [139] and is being used widely. However, as discussed earlier, WSDL and other web service description languages cannot be used to describe communication services. For providing semantics on the web, several languages have been recommended as well by the W3C. These languages are the Resource Description Framework (RDF) [138] and the Web Ontology Language (OWL) [137]. The main aim of developing all of these languages is to provide a framework for description, selection and composition of web services.

Similar demands of selection and composition of networking functionalities have been proposed by several researchers from the early 90s until today [103], [130], [120], [133], [81] and [66]. In the earlier works [103], [130] and [120], the authors considered only protocol based composition. Therefore, they did not concentrate on service description.

However, in recent works, authors expressed the necessity of a communication service description language as it is required by both service selection and service composition [133], [81], and [65]. The service description language which has been suggested in this thesis can fulfill these demands.

Protocol languages are programming languages to write networking protocols, algorithms or mechanisms. Examples of these languages are C [117] [118], C++ [2], C++ and Python [3], Standard ML [18], LOTOS [19], Erstelle [128], Esterel [21], RTAG [10], Prolac [71], SDL [128], and Morpheus [7]. However, these languages can not be used to describe the services (visible effects) offered by network protocols. The suggested language in this thesis can be used for that purpose.

The policies of a network administrator in an Ethane network can be defined by using the Pol-Eth language [28]. The language consists of a set of rules, where each of them has a condition and an action. For example, the following rule specifies that the user "ratul" is not allowed to communicate with the FTP server.

$$[(usrc = \text{``ratul''}) \wedge (protocol = \text{``ftp''}) \wedge (hdst = \text{``ftp-server''})] : deny;$$

However, using the Pol-Eth language, neither network offerings nor application requirements are described as the author does not provide the necessary vocabularies to describe them.

Web service description languages such as WSDL [139] and USDL [86] which are used to describe web services are not suitable for describing communication services as these two types of services differ in their basic properties. Web services are application/utility services which reside on the web and are accessed via Uniform Resource Locator (URL) addresses. On the other hand, communication services are located on every end- and intermediate nodes and can be accessed via well-defined interfaces. Communication services are composed to construct a protocol stack for communication association whereas web services are orchestrated to make a composite web service (i.e., a complex application) when the network stack is already available. The methods or operations that are exposed by web services are described using WSDL along with the message format and protocol details. As a communication service is offered by a self-contained building block in the service oriented network architectures (SONATE), the operations and message formats that are exposed by building blocks are hidden and only the resultant outcomes need to be described which necessitates a language to describe communication services.

3.2 Description and Language Requirements

This section begins by describing the challenges of defining a communication service description language. The requirements for the proposed language are discussed in Section 3.2.3 which have been derived by performing a literature survey of selection and composition approaches and system design principles (described in Section 3.2.2).

3.2.1 Communication Service Description Challenges

The goal is to define a communication service description language (which vocabularies to be developed for the language?, what should be the grammar for the language?) which is required for the selection (and composition).

The question is, why is it hard to specify such a language? The reasons are 1, to determine and specify the components for the language to describe communication services, application requirements, administrator policies, and network constraints so that suitable (and best) services are selected based on application requirements, administrator policies, and network constraints 2, the language (both vocabularies and grammars) must not be specific to any selection (and composition) method so that they are extensible and scalable and 3, all of the components in a selection (and composition) approach should speak a common language so that no intermediate translation is required.

3.2.2 Undertaking Approach to Tackle The Problems

The approach proposed in this thesis to tackle the description challenges was to analyze the selection and composition to derive the requirements for the description language. Based on the derived requirements, a communication service description language has been developed.

It is assumed that, in the selection and composition, a (partial) protocol graph for communication is constructed during design time, partial runtime, or in runtime by choosing a set of building blocks/micro-protocols/protocols from their repository based on the requirements from the application, net-

work, and administrator constraints. A model for the selection and composition is shown in Figure 1.1. The components of this model are:

Building Blocks: The functionalities in layered network architectures
are decomposed into a set of loosely-coupled building blocks so that they can
be flexibly composed whenever necessary. For example, the functionalities of
the TCP/IP protocol stack can be decomposed into a set of building blocks
such as segmentation, sequencing, "checksum" mechanism for error detection, "window-based flow control" for end-to-end flow control, "go-back-n"
for loss detection and loss reduction, "IPv4" for addressing, forwarding, encapsulation, "MAC" for medium access control functionalities, and "PHY"
for physical layer functionalities.

Storing the building blocks in a repository facilitates in reusing of existing
functionalities, removing them when they are obsolete, and flexible addition
of new functionalities. For example, whenever a building block which implements the "security" algorithm is proved to be "unsecure" such as Data
Encryption Standard (DES) [76][42], it should be removed.

During the selection and composition, the building blocks are composed
based on application requirements, administration policies, and network
constraints.

Application Requirements: Application can range from non-real time
(i.e., email) to real time (i.e., Voice over Internet Protocol (VoIP)). Each
of these applications has its specific requirement such as "email must be
reliable", "VoIP must be cheap" and, "e-Banking must be secure". Moreover,
the end-user might want to have customized requirements. For example, an
email user might want to have security and privacy for his business email.

Administration Policies: A network administrator can have different
types of policies. These policies are considered during the selection and
composition. For instance, when accessing the enterprise server from the

Intranet, a "no security" or a "weak in strength in terms of encryption key" security building block can be enabled so that the performance of the communication is not scaled down. However, when accessing the same enterprise server from the Internet, a "stronger in strength" security mechanism should be enabled to handle the threats from the intruders.

Network Constraints: The constraints of a (virtual) network are considered during the selection and composition. For example, in a low network bandwidth of an EDGE connection in a developing country such as Bangladesh, High Definition (HD) quality video can be prohibited. However, HD video can be allowed when the LTE network is used.

In the selection and composition, hardware constraints are also considered. For example, only the video with low resolution can be shown in the smart/cellular phone.

Selection and Composition (S&C): The building blocks are chosen and connected by a selection and composition method (S&C) considering application requirements, administration policies, and network constraints. The method can be either manual or automatic. In the first approach, building blocks are chosen and composed manually (sometimes assisted by a software) during design time by a protocol developer. In the second approach, the building blocks are selected and composed during runtime by an automatic composition method.

Protocol Graph: The resultant output of a S&C method is a protocol graph (a set of chosen and connected building blocks). For the communication association, either a "suitable" or "the best" protocol graph in terms of application requirements is utilized.

By performing a systematic literature survey of selection and composition approaches, the components that can be described to assist in providing flexibility in the selection and composition are obtained. The reasons of choosing literature survey as a methodology were 1, to identify existing knowledge (i.e., components of selection and composition that can be described), 2, and to derive new knowledge (i.e., in terms of describing the components for providing flexibility in selection and composition) [20].

The survey had three phases: 1, planning the review, 2, conducting the review, and 3, reporting the review as suggested by Barbara Kitchenham [70].

	Adaptive	DaCaPO	ANA	NENA	FoG
Available components					
Application/user requirements	yes	yes	yes	yes	yes
Network properties	yes	yes (i.e., transport properties)	yes	yes	yes
Administrator policies	yes			yes	yes
Network/hardware constraints	yes		yes	yes	yes
Dependencies	Requires knowledge of the predecessor(s)	Only data dependency is considered	N/A	Static configuration	Pre-configured
Taxonomy/ontologies specification	no	no	no	no	yes (architecture specific)
BB-interface	yes	Yes (module properties)	Yes (FB, Compartment)	yes (BB, Netlet)	yes (Gates)
PG-interface	yes	yes	yes	yes	yes
Composite service	yes	yes	yes	yes	yes
Architectural drawbacks					
Drawbacks	Specific to multimedia application and higher layer protocols	Only considered transport functionalities	Dependency solution is not available	Every application requires one pre-composed PG	Only consider routing functions

Table 3.2 Comparison of different network architectures

In the planning phase, the review objective, "what to describe in selection and composition approaches?" and the primary sources were identified. Considering the maturity of the architectures in terms of their age, five approaches were selected to review: Adaptive [103][104][102], DaCaPO

[129][130], ANA [127][63], NENA [75][53] and, FoG [73][74]. The approaches Adaptive, and DaCaPO were developed in the beginning of the 1990s. ANA is a result of an EU project which started in 2006. NENA is an outcome of two simultaneously running projects (an EU project 4WARD and a German-based project G-LAB) which started in 2008. FoG is an output of a German-based project which started in 2009. The availability of a prototype and/or a demonstration helps to understand the approach. Even though the earlier approaches, such as Adaptive and DaCaPO, have no prototype or demonstration, whereas each of the newer approaches, such as ANA, NENA, and FoG, have either one or both of them.

In the conducting phase, the research question was reviewed and reformulated as "what are the components of selection and composition approaches that can be described (describable)". To gather the answer, each primary study was reviewed to retrieve its design components. The result of the review is reported in Table 3.2.

In this work, it is proposed that all of the (both common and uncommon) design components of the studied approaches as depicted in Table 3.2 can be described. These components can be explained as follows:

Different types of application requirements: Selection and composition deals with different types of application requirements. According to ITU-T Recommendation Y.1541, there can be different classes of applications such as 0, real-time, jitter sensitive, high interaction (multimedia conferencing, VoIP, broadcast video, telephony), 1, real-time, jitter sensitive, interactive, 2, transaction data, highly interactive (signaling), 3, transaction data, interactive, 4, low loss only (bulk data, multi-media streaming, short transactions), 5, and traditional application of default IP networks [61]. Application can also be distinguished into four types according to their traffic classes such as 1, elastic non-interactive (file download, email) 2, elastic interactive (telnet, web browsing) 3, non-elastic non-interactive (video-on-demand, radio broadcast), and 4, non-elastic interactive (video chat, online gaming, VoIP) [115]. Moreover, an end-user may have customized requirements. For example, a VoIP user might want to have security and privacy for his application.

Description of different user requirements: During the selection and composition, end-users are given the possibility to add, delete and update their application requirements.

Different network properties: Network properties are measured or estimated values for an end-to-end network connection (e.g., 10 Mbps WLAN, 1 Gbps Ethernet). Different types of networks (i.e., Ethernet, WLAN, mobile) might be used from one end to another end. The aggregated properties of those networks such as end-to-end delay, bandwidth and loss ratio are considered during the selection and composition.

Different administrator policies: Different networks have different administration policies. In the selection and composition approaches including Adaptive, NENA, and FoG, the policies from the network administrator considered during the selection and composition process. For example, a network administrator might specify that security must be enabled when using a particular network to keep the users of that network safe and secure.

Different network/hardware constraints: The constraints of a (virtual) network are considered during the selection and composition. For example, in a low network bandwidth of an EDGE connection in a developing country such as India, High Definition (HD) quality video can be prohibited. These network constraints can be implemented and used by the service providers such as O2, Deutsche Telekom, Vodafone. Moreover, hardware constraints are also considered during the selection and composition. For example, only the video with low resolution can be shown in the smart/cellular phone.

Dependencies: In the selection and composition, dependencies can be between BBs, between BB services, between a BB and a BB service. There can be multiple types of dependencies such as mutual exclusion (two BBs must not run in parallel), one BB requires another BB. However, currently the dependencies between the BBs are statically configured which has negative impact on scaling (how many BB with statically defined dependencies can be handled?).

Taxonomy specification: The taxonomy of the resultant effects of a building block is only specified in the FoG approach. However, as they consider only routing functionalities, their defined taxonomy is limited in scope.

PG-interface: In the selection and composition, an application communicates with a protocol graph through a PG-interface. However, the interface is tightly coupled with both the application and the PG. Therefore, to use the interface, an application requires knowledge about the available network functionalities.

BB-interface: The building blocks are connected with each other by using a BB-interface in the selection and composition.

Composite service: All of the approaches produce protocol graphs, thus providing service to the application.

To recapitulate, by studying the selection and composition approaches, the architectural components (as described above) are derived. However, those components lack in providing flexibility and re-usability. The properties of those components are: 1, the services (capabilities, outcome or resultant effects) of the building blocks and the protocol-graphs are not specified, hence, they are not reusable. 2, the inputs of the selection and composition including application requirements, network properties, administration policies, and network/hardware constraints are not specified, therefore, they cannot express their demand from the network. 3, there is a lack of a communication service description language including a taxonomy/ontology so that both inputs and outputs of the selection and composition can be specified.

3.2.3 Requirements for the Proposed Language

Based on the result of the literature survey (as described before) and system design principles, the requirements for the description language have been elicited as follows. The requirements are categorized as mandatory and optional. Mandatory requirements must be fulfilled by the language and optional requirements are best practices.

3.2.3.1 Mandatory Requirements

Able to describe the components in a modular basis: The language must be able to describe all of the aforementioned components of selection and composition considering modularity design principle so that modification of the description of one component does not require to change the description of another component [14]. A modular design not only reduces the complexity but also increases the parallel development of different components of a system [94].

The language should be capable of hiding implementation details: D. L. Parnas et. al. proved that the re-usability of a software module can be enhanced with information hiding [90]. In a selection and composition approach, a building block should be reused in constructing a protocol graph and an already constructed protocol graph should be reused in communication association. Therefore, the language to be developed should hide the internal implementation details of a building block or a protocol graph to increase re-usability.

No predecessor/successor knowledge should be required: In NENA, as the PG is composed during design time, static configuration of dependency is done. Similarly in the Adaptive approach, dependencies between different BBs are implemented using C++ properties such as encapsulation, dynamic binding, and inheritance [22]. However, this approach assumes that the developer has the knowledge of the predecessor classes. This hard assumption might fail for a new developer or for an experienced developer when the number of classes increases. This implies the requirement for the language that both new and experienced developers should be able to describe a communication service without having knowledge of its predecessor or successor.

Able to describe all types of communication functionalities: The architecture in the Adaptive approach is specific to multimedia application and higher layer protocols [102]. In FoG, only application (i.e., transcoding), and routing functionalities are taken into account [135]. The language to be developed should be able to describe different ranges of communication functionalities.

Independent from a particular selection and composition mechanism: A key to a good design is functional independence of modules which reduces complexity, increases maintainability, and supports parallel development [94]. Therefore, the language to be developed should not be specific to any selection, composition, selection and composition mechanism so that both of them can be evolved in a parallel manner. There are different types of selection and composition methods based on their time of execution, such as design time, partial runtime, and runtime. The netlet in NENA, the template in SONATE, and the evolutionary approach in SONATE are examples of design time, partial runtime and runtime composition approaches respectively. DaCaPO is also seen as a runtime composition approach [130]. The language to be developed should not be specific to a particular composition approach so that it can also be used by a newly developed approach.

Supporting selection and composition of building blocks: The aim of a selection and composition approach is to select and compose building blocks based on inputs such as application requirements, network constraints, and administration requirements. The language to be proposed should be able to describe all of the inputs and the capabilities of building blocks so that the building blocks can be selected and composed.

Extensibility: The capabilities of the network are increasing day-by-day with new protocols (for example, encryption, and compression algorithms), storage capacity, and computational power (Moore's law [80]). The requirements of an application have also been changing. So, developing a language with the principle "one size fits all" is not appropriate. That is why, the description language must be extensible with new vocabularies and grammars so that new requirements and functionalities can be described.

Capable of describing different types of requirements: In the selection and composition, some of the application requirements must be guaranteed by a building block / protocol graph. For example, the "Security" and "ReliableDelivery" requirements of a safety critical application (for instance, monitoring an implanted medical device, flight control) must be guaranteed whereas the "UsageCost" for such an application can be an optional requirement. Using the language, it should be possible to specify both guaranteed (mandatory) and non-guaranteed (optional) requirements so that (most) suitable building blocks and protocol graphs can be selected.

By using mandatory requirements, suitable building blocks can be chosen for constructing protocol graphs and suitable protocol graphs can be selected for a communication association. By using optional requirements, the most appropriate building block based on application requirements can be selected to compose protocol graphs and the most appropriate protocol graph can be selected for a communication association.

Able to aggregate end-to-end properties: To assist in selection and composition process of building blocks or protocol graphs, end-to-end properties of different networks should be aggregated. The aggregated properties of those networks such as end-to-end delay, bandwidth and loss ratio should be described as optional as they are highly dynamic and cannot be guaranteed.

Capable of describing dependency without compromising flexibility: Sometimes tight coupling cannot be avoided to optimize efficiency, however, it decreases re-usability benefits [26]. The dependency description is a consequence of tight-coupling and should be described as optional as they hinder flexibility. The reason for describing dependency is that, whenever efficiency is important for an application, the dependency description can be utilized. Moreover, the types of dependencies should be expressed based on their significance such as "must be fulfilled" or "best practices". In addition, if there is any dependency pattern such as predecessor-successor, mutual exclusion or must not run in parallel, they should also be described.

Effects on the properties of building blocks: In a selection and composition approach such as NENA, a building block augments effects on the properties such as addition, subtraction, multiplication, or division. How to describe those augmented effects? Whenever a message is sent to the network using a protocol graph, each building block in the protocol graph which processes that message, adds processing delay. Moreover, a

building block might also add some information into the message so that
the message can be handled properly in the receiving side which increases
the size of the message. For example, a CRC building block adds checksum
with the message to enable checking of the message in terms of error on the
receiving side. Therefore, the requirement is to find out and describe those
effects of a building block.

Independent from the granularity of building blocks: Most of the
selection and composition approaches including NENA and ANA, both fine-
grained and coarse-grained building blocks are considered. The language
should not be specific to any particular granularity of building blocks and
can describe their both fine-grained (i.e., hamming code) and coarse-grained
functionalities (i.e., TCP).

Describing the service independent on their location: In FoG,
building blocks reside on the end-node and middle boxes. In NENA, protocol
graphs (netlets) reside mainly on the end-nodes. Therefore, in selection and
composition approaches, both building blocks and protocol graphs can be
placed on end nodes, middle boxes (e.g., network router), or on every node
on the network. The language should be capable of describing their services
wherever they are.

Independent from Application Programming Interface (API):
In composition approaches including NENA, and ANA, an Application Programming Interface (API) is located between an application, and the selection and composition engine, and is used to send an application's requirement to the engine so that a protocol graph can be constructed by selecting
and composing building blocks. The language to be developed should not
be specific to any particular API so that future APIs will be able to use the
language.

Aggregation of BB effects: In SONATE and NENA, a protocol graph is an ordered set of building blocks. For selecting suitable and the best protocol graph, the aggregation of BB effects is required. The language to be developed should support the aggregation of those effects.

All components must be able to speak the same language: The efficiency and productivity of a selection and composition approach can be improved if all of the components speak the same language. Moreover, when several languages are used, they might not be fully compatible to each other. Efficiency (in terms of selection and composition time) can be increased as no extra module (including its interfaces and protocols) is required to translate the description from one language to another language. Similarly, the productivity can also be improved as it is not necessary for an application developer to learn a new language to describe a networking component (i.e., for describing administration policies and networking constraints).

3.2.3.2 Optional Requirements

Mutation of a protocol graph to generate a new protocol graph: The re-usability of a software module is enhanced if it is mutable to make another module with minor modification [77]. Similarly, the re-usability of a protocol graph (is seen as a composed module of building blocks) can be enhanced by providing a possibility of modification. The modification can be done easily if a protocol graph can be automatically described from the selected building blocks (based on application requirements and/or network conditions).

Usability of the description language: Usability may be considered before developing a system [56]. In selection and composition approaches, end-users are given the possibility to add, delete, and update their application requirements. Therefore, those requirements should be expressed in a format which is usable in terms of "easy to learn", "efficient to use", "easy to remember", "few errors", and "subjectively pleasing" as elicited by Jakob Nielson [85].

Selection of the most appropriate protocol graph: NENA selects the most appropriate protocol graph (netlet) based on an application requirement during runtime [133]. Similarly, DaCaPO chooses the best protocol for the configuration according to an application requirement [130]. The description language to be developed could support this task.

Supports rating of effects: Composition approaches including NENA, different mechanisms can be used to rate the capabilities of building blocks and protocol graphs. The effects may be expressed using the language in such a way so that any rating mechanism can access those effects (i.e., static input (benchmarking) and dynamic inputs (benchmarking based on dynamically monitored information)) and rate them.

Independent from objective function: In selection and composition approaches including NENA, an objective function is used to rate a service based on the effects (and especially on their rating) in order to select the best building block or protocol graph. A description language for the building block or protocol graph may not be dependent on any objective function.

Assists in transparent selection and composition: In NENA, building blocks are selected and composed during design time to create a protocol graph (netlet) where a protocol developer involves with the complexities of selection and composition (may get assisted by a software). This requires manual effort and cost. To reduce that, the language may support transparent selection and composition of building blocks based on the application requirements to get application/protocol developers rid of complexity of selection and composition.

Supports verification and validation: Selection and composition approaches including NENA (when a composition software is used), and ANA, syntactic or semantic verification and validation mechanisms are used to prove the correctness of statically or dynamically composed BBs (i.e., a protocol graph). A language to be developed may assist in those tasks, but, might not be specific to those mechanisms.

Supports heterogeneity: The selection and composition approaches may support different types of networks simultaneously. To deal with such a heterogeneity, different types of negotiation methods (i.e., priori, on demand) can be utilized. The potential language may support heterogeneity by describing all of the effects which are necessary for negotiation.

In the following section, a communication service description language is proposed by considering the aforementioned mandatory and optional requirements. The earlier versions of the language have been presented in the ITU Kleidoscope [66] and NoF conference [68]. In the NoF conference, the paper has been nominated for the best paper award [23]. The matured version of the language has been selected by ITU as a standardization candidate [4].

3.3 Solution: Communication Service Description Language (CSDL)

The goal of developing the communication service description language is to assist in selecting and composing (S&C) building blocks to generate a protocol graph. Towards this goal, the language must be able to describe fine-grained functionalities (i.e., the capacities or capabilities of a building block), constraints from the network, policies from the administrator and requirements from the application. Moreover, the output of the selection and composition (S&C) engine is a protocol graph which should also be described using the same language as shown in Figure 1.2. The selection of a suitable, or the best, coarse-grained service requires the description of requirements and offerings, as shown in Figure 1.3, should also be described without changing the language.

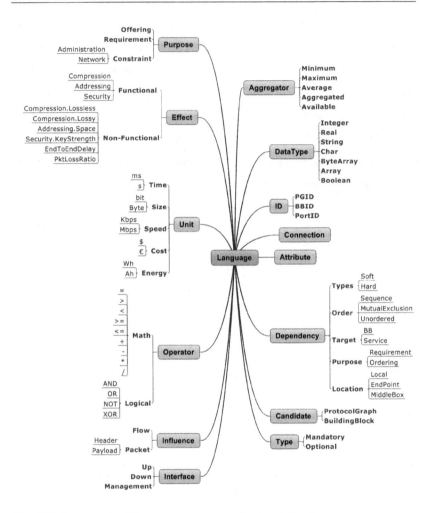

Fig. 3.2 Components of the communication service description language

All of these requirements, constraints, and offerings (i.e., the *Purpose*
of description) require specifications of effects, influence, interfaces, data
types, and dependencies. Effects and interfaces are required to hide internal

implementation mechanism from an application or a user and show only the parts that are required during selection and composition. Whether a building block or a service influences a header of a packet, the payload of a packet or the flow needs to be known during service selection and composition. During service composition, the compatibility of the connections between interfaces is checked using data types. An interface can only accept a connection from the building block X if the building block offers data of a particular type [105]. Dependencies are required to assist the selection and composition process. The components of the language are shown in Figure 3.2.

3.3.1 Effects

The communication service of a building block, or a protocol graph (i.e., the *Candidate* for description) is described by a set of effects. The effects of a communication service can be requested by an application developer. An ontology for effects to represent communication services is discussed in [65] and described in detail here. For matching requirements and offerings, each effect should have a unique name used as a unique identifier which is be described by using *Effect*.

Effects can either be **functional** or **non-functional** as shown in Figure 3.2. The functional capabilities of a building block or a protocol graph are exposed using functional effects and their QoS (Quality of Service) capabilities are expressed using non-functional effects. For example, when any building block implements a routing protocol such as Open Shortest Path First (OSPF) or Routing Information Protocol (RIP), then it provides the functional effect routing in general as it has the capability to gather data

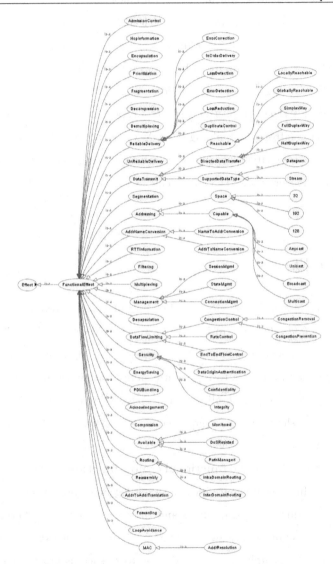

Fig. 3.3 A taxonomy of functional effects

from neighboring nodes (destination address, hop count, next router) to take routing decision. More specifically, those protocols have the capability to gather data and route packets within a single administrative domain. Thus, those protocols provide the effect IntraDomainRouting. Similarly, as BGP (Border Gateway Protocol) has the capability to gather data and route packets between different administrative domains, it provides the functional effect InterDomainRouting. End-to-end delay, bandwidth, and lossratio are some examples of non-functional effects. Even though encryption is seen as a functional effect as it describes a functionality, however, the key length (256 bits) of the AES256 encryption building block is seen as a non-functional effect as it describes the quality of that functionality.

Functional Effects

A taxonomy for the functional effects has been constructed as shown in Figure 3.3. The methodology of building the taxonomy was to review the related literatures. Moreover, communication protocols of different OSI layers have also been reviewed to verify whether the claimed effect can really be provided by the protocol (or a micro-protocol).

Syntactically, a functional effect is expressed by its name

```
NameOfFunctionalEffect
```

Addressing is probably the most widely used functional effect. Currently, IPv4 and IPv6 protocols are used to provide the effect by identifying the source device, and the destination device.

In general, **security** [122] is a functional effect. It is seen from Figure 3.3 that effects may be hierarchical. The security effect consists of three effects: Confidentiality, Integrity, and DataOriginAuthentication. Mechanisms which use symmetric and asymmetric signatures for ensuring that the received data has been originated by the intended communication partner and not been altered by the intruder, provide the effect of DataOriginAuthentication. For example, the X.509 certificate offers the effect of DataOriginAuthentication. Mechanisms which are used to detect that the message has not been altered during transmission provide the effect of Integrity. An example of such a mechanism is hash function. Some mechanisms such as encryption [13][33] provide the effect of confidentiality which ensure that only the authenticated user can access the message.

ReliableDelivery [13][33][17][142] is a functional effect which is provided by the mechanisms that ensure that the data arrived in the destination in order and without having loss and error. Currently, the coarse-grained Transmission Control Protocol (TCP) offers the ReliableDelivery effect. However, the effect can also be provided by the User Datagram Protocol (UDP) when additional mechanisms are used. Fine-grained mechanisms such as Repetition code, Cyclic Redundancy Check (CRC), Parity Check, Checksum, and Error Correcting Codes are used to detect errors, thus, providing the effect of ErrorDetection [33][142]. Acknowledgment and retransmission mechanisms (which re-send loss and erroneous packets) provide the effects ErrorControl and ErrorCorrection. Retransmission and Forward Error Correction (FEC) (adds redundant data into the packet) mechanisms which offer ErrorCorrection effect can be distinguished based on their quality attribute. Whereas retransmission mechanisms can correct 100% error, FEC mechanisms can correct specific amount of errors. For example, Hamming (7,4) code can correct any single bit error. Building blocks which implement different Automatic Repeat reQuest (ARQ) methods such as Stop-and-Wait ARQ, Go-Back-N ARQ, Selective Repeat ARQ can correct 100% of the error. However, repetition code, hamming code, Reed-Solomon code, multi-dimensional parity-check code, turbo codes, and Hybrid ARQ (combination of both reatransmission and FEC mechanisms) can correct specific amounts of error. Retransmission and FEC mechanisms can also be distinguished based on whether they can either offer ErrorCorrection or LossDetection effect or they can offer both of them. Whereas retransmission mechanisms can offer both of the effects, FEC mechanism can only offer ErrorCorrection effect. Retransmission mechanisms ([103][33][51][122]) such as ARQ re-sends erroneous or lost packets, thus providing the effect of LossDetection [22], and ErrorCorrection. The InOrderDelivery effect [13][103][33][142] [51][122] is provided by those mechanisms which ensure that the packets are delivered in the same sequence as they are transmitted. The mechanism which provides the DuplicateControl effect [103] ensures that all duplicate packets are recognized and discarded. Usually, by using sequence numbers, the mechanism which provides InOrderDelivery effect also offers DuplicateControl effect.

Building blocks where mechanisms to control the flow of the data are implemented, offer the effect of **FlowControl**. The mechanisms such as the stop-and-wait ARQ and the sliding window protocol which avoid overwhelming the receiver from unnecessary packet, provide the effect of EndToEndFlowControl [13][103][33][51]. Mechanisms which are either used to prevent the congestion before it has occurred or remove after their occurrence provide CongestionControl effect. In the earlier case, one or several of the mechanisms such as retransmission policy, window policy, acknowledgment policy, discarding policy, and admission policy offer the CongestionPrevention effect [13][33][51]. In the later case, the mechanisms such as back pressure, choke packet, implicit signaling, and explicit signaling provide Congestion Removal effect. The mechanisms which provide CongestionControl effect in TCP are slow start (exponential increase), congestion avoidance (additive increase), and congestion detection (multiplicative decrease). The building blocks which implement the mechanisms to maintain the rate of data flow entering into the network provide the RateControl effect.

When a building block or a protocol graph has the ability to transfer data from one node to another, the effect is called here **DataTransmission**. Reachability is a functional effect, the capability of a node to reach another node in the Intranet (LocalReachability) or Internet (GlobalRechability). A building block or a protocol graph might be able to transmit a stream or a datagram. A stream is a flow of data which is sent to the receiver conforming reliability. A datagram, a fixed length packet, is usually sent to the destination without ensuring reliability. A building block or a protocol graph can transmit data in one way (Simplex), two ways but one way at one time (HalfDuplex), and two ways simultaneously (FullDuplex).

The effect **"Availability"** is offered when a mechanism ensures that the node or service is still accessible even after the congested path or Denial of Service (DoS) attack. "Monitoring" is an effect which is provided when the underlying mechanism monitors the network. The effect "PathManagement" is offered when the mechanisms ensure to use alternative paths. Examples of those mechanisms are multihoming [142] and loadsharing. In multihoming, several networks from different service providers are connected to a host, but, only one path (network) is active at one time. In loadsharing, two or more paths can be active simultaneously. The mechanisms which offer the "PathManagement" effect usually depend on the mechanisms which offer the "Monitoring" effect.

Certain mechanisms are used to reduce the size of the data, header or both, thus provide the **Compression** [13][33] effect. The same mechanisms which provide the "Compression" effect, also provide a "Decompression" effect to get back the original data with certain loss or no loss.

Certain mechanisms in the routing protocols are used to avoid loop during routing data. These protocols then provide the effect of **"LoopAvoidance"** as well.

Time-To-Live (TTL) is used to count the number of hops (routers) between a source and a destination and provides the effect **"HopCount"**.

The "ping" command can count the Round-Trip-Time (RTT) between the source and the destination thus provide the effect of **"RTTInformation"**. The output of the effect can be provided with additional data such as aggregated minimum, average, maximum and maximum deviation.

When a mechanism is implemented to manage the state of the resource (BB or PG), session and connection, the mechanism provides the effect of **"Management"** in general. "StateMgmt" [122] is an effect which is provided when the underlying mechanism is used to manage the operational, usage, administrative, and power consumption state of a resource [60]. "SessionMgmt" [51] is an effect which is provided by mechanisms such as cookies in web browsers, x session manager in desktop systems, to maintain the state of a session. "ConnectionMgmt" [103][93] is an effect which is offered when a BB or PG is responsible for the connection establishment, the connection persistence, and the connection termination with the communication partner.

If a mechanism has no capability to deliver the message to the destination without loss and error, then it offers the **"UnReliableDelivery"** [103] effect. The coase-grained building block User Datagram Protocol (UDP) offers that effect.

The **"Forwarding"** [135][33][122][126] effect is provided by the protocol or mechanism which sends the packet to the next building block in SONATE, the subsequent gate in FoG, or the succeeding network node.

The **"AddrNameConversion"** [103] effect is offered by the protocol or mechanism which can convert from a domain name to an IP address providing the effect of "NameToAddrConversion" and the other way around providing the effect of "AddrToNameConversion" similar to the Domain Name System (DNS).

The effect **"Acknowledgment"** [103] is provided by the mechanism which ensures that the feedback about reception of the packet is sent to the sender. The effect is usually necessary for those mechanisms which provide LossDetection effect.

The effect **"AdmissionControl"** [122] is offered by the mechanism which checks the availability of the shared resources such as CPU, memory, bandwidth and accept, modify or reject the new connection requests [116].

The effect **"Encapsulation"** [33] is provided by the mechanism which takes a packet and encapsulates that packet into a new packet by adding some more information which is necessary during decapsulation (Decapsulation effect). For example, the Internet Control Message Protocol (ICMP) which is used by the ping utility is encapsulated at first in the IP packet, the IP packet is then encapsulated in the Ethernet frame and then the Ethernet frame is sent to the next node.

The effect **"Filtering"** [122] is offered by the mechanisms including Packet Filtering (PF) or stateful inspection which examine incoming packets by matching the contents of the packet (both header and the data) with the predefined rules and allow them to pass or block. The mechanisms which provide the "Filtering" effect also provides a "Security" effect.

The effect **"MAC"** [33] is provided when a building block implements the functionalities of the medium access control (MAC) protocol such as address resolution. "AddrResolution" is an effect where an IP address is resolved to an Ethernet address with the Address Resolution protocol (ARP), and an

Ethernet address is translated to an IP address with the Reverse Address Translation protocol(RARP).

The effect **"AddrToAddrTranslation"** [12] is provided by a mechanism which can convert from one type of address to another type of address [16][112] such as from IPv4 address to IPv6 address and vice versa.

The **"Multiplexing"** [122] effect is provided by a mechanism or a device which takes several analog signals or digital data streams and converts that into a single one to transfer through a shared medium. The opposite effect is "Demultiplexing" which is provided by usually the same mechanism or device which provides "Multiplexing" effect to return back multiple analog signals or digital data streams.

The **"PDUBundling"** [142] effect is provided by the mechanism which sends several Protocol Data Units (PDUs) into a single PDU to reduce overhead [15].

The effect **"Segmentation"** is provided by the mechanism which accepts a data stream and breaks that stream into a set of fixed size packets called segments. The effect **"Fragmentation"** is offered by the mechanism which accepts a fixed size packet and breaks that into another fixed size packet called frame. The opposite effect of "Segmentation" and "Fragmentation" is **"Reassembly"** which recombines the fragmented or segmented packet.

The effect **"Prioritization"** is provided by the mechanism which ensures that certain type of traffic such as voice is given priority over another type of traffic such as best effort as specified in IEEE 802.11e specification.

The effect **"EnergySaving"** is provided by the mechanism which ensures that usage energies are saved in an optimal way.

Non-functional Effects

A taxonomy for the non-functional effects has been constructed as shown in Figure 3.4. The methodology of building the taxonomy was to review the related literature. Moreover, communication protocols of different OSI layers have also been reviewed to verify whether the claimed effect can really be provided by the protocol (or a micro-protocol).

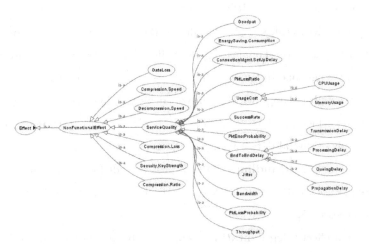

Fig. 3.4 A taxonomy of non-functional effects

Non-functional effects are related to functional effects and describe the qualities of the underlying functionalities. For example, a data size reduction algorithm provides the functional effect "compression". But, the power or ratio of a compression algorithm is seen as a non-functional effect. Such a non-functional effect is expressed in a hierarchical order.

NameOfFunctionalEffect.NameOfNonFunctionalEffect

However, the hierarchy is optional when a non-functional effect is not related to a functional-effect. In such a case, a non-functional effect is represented by its name

NameOfNonFunctionalEffect

The compression mechanisms can be lossless or lossy. As the name indicates, lossless compression methods which provide the **Compression.Lossless** effect do not lose any data during compression or decompression. These methods are Run-length encoding, Lempel-Ziv (LZ78), Lempel-Ziv-Welch (LZW), DEFLATE, bzip2, Lemple-Ziv-Markov chain algorithm (LZMA), Lempel-Ziv-Oberhumer (LZO), Statistical Lempel Ziv, MPEG-4 Audio Lossless Coding (ALS), MPEG-4 Scalable Lossless Coding (SLS). Lossy compression methods which offer the **Compression.Lossy** effect, on the other hand, sacrifice some loss of data by using the weakness of human visibility perception and psycho acoustics. Examples of lossy compression methods are Cartesian Perceptual Compression (CPC), fractal compression, wavelet compression, H.264, JPEG and MP3. Some mechanisms can be configured with either the Compression.Lossless or the Compression.Lossy effect. For example, JBIG2, JPEG 2000, JPEG extended range (JPEG XR) and Progressive Graphics File (PGF).

The processing time that is necessary to compress a particular amount of data is the speed of the compression algorithm and can be provided as the effect **Compression.Speed**. On the other hand, the time that is necessary to retrieve the original data from the compressed data is the speed of the decompression algorithm and can be provided as the **Decompression.Speed** effect.

The power of a compression algorithm is provided by the effect **Compression.Ratio** and is the ratio of the data size after the compression has applied and its original size before the compression has applied.

Encryption is a mechanism which provides the functional effect of "Security". However, the strength of an encryption algorithm which is measured by its key length provides the non-functional effect of **Security.KeyStrength**.

The quality of a service is seen as a non-functional effect and is expressed by **ServiceQuality**. In this case, services can be provided by fine-grained building blocks, coarse-grained building blocks, or composition of building blocks (i.e., protocol graph). Usually, the ServiceQuality effect of a composed protocol graph is the summation of the value of the effect of each involved building block. For example, the effect **ProcessingDelay** of a protocol graph is the summation of the ProcessingDelay of each individual building block.

The effect "UsageCost" is the cost for the use of a service which is made up of "CPUUsage" and "MemoryUsage".

The ratio of the number of loss packets and the total number of sent packets is the loss ratio and can be provided as the effect "PktLossRatio". The opposite effect is the "SuccessRate" which is the ratio of the number of successfully arrived packets and the total number of sent packets.

The latency to set up a connection between the source and the destination is provided as the effect **ConnectionMgmt.SetUpDelay**.

Considering different ideal scenarios (which is called benchmarking), the probability of packet loss can be calculated and offered as the effect "Pkt-LossProbability".

The time it takes for a packet to be transmitted by the sender and to be accepted by the receiver in one way direction is called end-to-end delay and can be provided as an effect **EndtoEndDelay**. The end-to-end delay is the summation of all the delays between the sender and receiver. These delays are transmission delay, propagation delay, queuing delay, processing delay, and provided as the effects "TransmissionDelay", "PropagationDelay", "QueingDelay", and "ProcessingDelay" respectively. Usually, every building block and network routers provide all of these effects. The time requires to place all of the bits of a packet into the transmission medium (in case of routers), or to forward a packet into the sending port (in case of building block) is the transmission delay. The time it requires for a packet to propagate to the next building block or to the next router is the propagation delay. Before sending, the packets are usually kept in the buffers (sometimes called queue). The time it requires for a packet to wait in the queue before being transmitted is the "QueingDelay". The time it takes for a router or a building block to process a packet, is the "ProcessingDelay". Usually, they read the header of a packet to know the destination address and the port to forward the packet. Sometimes, they also read the content of a packet to investigate security breaches.

The end-to-end delay variation between the sender and the receiver is called packet delay variation or jitter and can be expressed by the effect **"Jitter"**.

The amount of energy that is consumed by a building block or a protocol graph to provide a service is called energy consumption and is offered as the effect **EnergySaving.Consumption.**

The actual data rate of an application is the goodput and is provided as the effect **Goodput**. In the OSI model, goodput is measured in the application layer. The average rate of successful data message delivery over a communication channel is throughput and is provided as the effect **Throughput**. The maximum throughput of a communication channel is Bandwidth and is offered as the effect **Bandwidth.**

Some effects are listed in functional-effects taxonomies in this thesis, however, these effects are categorized as quality parameters (non-functional) in other domains including software-engineering. These effects are Security, Availability, and ReliableDelivery. Both ISO/IEC 25010 [5] and OASIS [69] included all of these three parameters in their quality model. The reason for defining those effects as functional in this thesis is that they represent functionalities (not quality attributes) of a building block or a protocol graph.

Though some effects such as Addressing.Space and Addressing.Capable that are defined as functional effects, they may also be defined as non-functional effects. As discussed before, *Addressing* is a functional effect. However, the qualities of addressing such as addressing space (**Addressing.Space**) and capabilities of addressing (**Addressing.Capable**) can be seen as both functional and non-functional effects as they represent both functionalities *Addressing = true*, *Addressing = true* and qualities of functionalities *Addressing = 32Bit*, *Addressing = 128Bit* in terms of address space. IPv4 provides the the effect of **32 Bit** and IPv6 provides **128 Bit**. When other new mechanisms such as LOC/ID Split are implemented, the effect of that mechanism could also be described by their address space (the number of bits that are used by them). Specifying mechanism related information in the taxonomy such as 32 bit address space for IPv4 or 128 bit address space for IPv6 is not recommended as it hinders transparency. However, in this case, an application developer can either request for "Addressing" in general or can ask for a specific space of addressing to be more specific. An addressing mechanism might be capable of addressing a single host, multiple hosts, any host or all hosts thus provides the effects of **UniCast**, **MultiCast**, **AnyCast**, and **BroadCast** respectively.

Some of the non-functional effects can be used during the evaluation process of a service or a set of services. Examples of those effects are success rate, delay, jitter and loss ratio. Such an effect is expressed by only its name

```
NameOfNonFunctionalEffect
```

These effects can be used for proper functioning of a building block or a service. For example, the success rate, and the loss ratio can be used by a retransmission building block to calculate the number of packets to retransmit.

Integrating or removing a building block or a service can result in different values of those effects. For example, CPU-usage can reach higher values when a complex building block is added.

3.3.2 Operators

Both mathematical and logical operators are required to describe requirements and offerings. These operators are necessary for comparing between the requirements and offerings. An example of a requirement is $\{(Bandwidth = 2Mbps)OR(Delay = 100ms)\}$. This says that Bandwidth must be equal to 2Mbps or delay must be equal to 100ms. Requirements are fulfilled when one of these two conditions is fulfilled.

Moreover, the operators are used for addition, subtraction, multiplication and division of the values of effects. For example, introducing and using a retransmission building block into a protocol graph adds the delay.

3.3.3 Units

Units are necessary to match requirements and offerings. These units can be organized based on their usage. For example, a time unit is used to measure the delay of a packet, a size unit is used to indicate the size of a packet, a speed unit calculates the access bandwidth, cost measures the cost, and energy indicates the energy consumption of a device or equipment. For instance, an application requirement can be $\{Cost < 0.02\$\}$.

3.3.4 Attributes

An attribute, a value for an effect in addition to its unit, is used to compare requirements and offerings. For example, the attribute for the application requirement $\{Cost < 0.02\$\}$ is 0.02$. The value can be assigned or calculated by using a *Formula* (i.e., mathematical equation). The ProcessingDelay of a building block can be measured and assigned when the environmental conditions are known (for example, OS, processing power, and memory). When retransmission BB is used to provide "ReliableDelivery" service, the DataRate effect of such a building block could be calculated by using the following formula

```
<Attribute Unit="bit/s">
<Formula Type="python">if retransmitpacket == 1: DataRate =
    DataRate + (PacketSize/Time) else: DataRate</Formula>
</Attribute>
```

Moreover, attributes could be predicted based on the history of network usage. In the following, an example is provided for estimated DataRate of a network during off peak and peak hours.

```
<Attribute Unit="Mbit/s">
<Formula Type="python">if time == offpeak: DataRate = 100
    else: DataRate = 10</Formula>
</Attribute>
```

3.3.5 ID

Every description candidate including a building block and a protocol graph
must have unique identifier (ID) so that they can be searched and used. Each
protocol graph, a composition of building blocks, is identified by a PGID.
A building block can have several interfaces which are identified by using
PortIDs. During composition, PortIDs are necessary to make *Connections*
between building blocks where each building block is identified by a BBID.

3.3.6 Influence

During the selection and composition process, it is necessary to know
whether a mechanism modifies a flow of packets, a single packet, the header
part of the packet or the payload of the packet. For example, the *RTTEstimator* service does not change the content of a packet (i.e. does not add any
information to the header or to the payload). The details of the *RTTEstimator* service are described in Section 3.3.13. On the contrary, the compression
and the security services change the size of a flow of packets.

3.3.7 Interface

Effects are offered through the interfaces (ports) and must also be accessed
by using interfaces which hide the implementation details. For obtaining an
effect, an application needs to know only the unique name and type of the
interface through which a particular effect is provided [105]. Examples of
interfaces are up, down, and management.

3.3.8 DataType

An effect is provided and offered when it receives the data of a specific *DataType*. For example, the Compression effect can only be provided when it receives data in a byte array format. Moreover, an interface is associated with a specific *DataType*. Selection and composition mechanisms require compatibility checking between/among services. Compatibility can be checked by using datatypes.

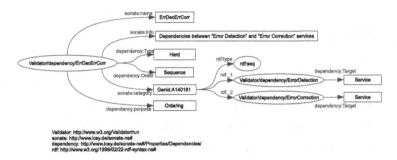

Fig. 3.5 Description of dependencies between error detection and error correction

3.3.9 Dependencies

During service composition, dependencies are considered to prepare a fully functional service. These dependencies can be between building blocks, between services, and between a building block and a service. The "Target" represents these dependency targets (BB and Service). Dependencies can be described using purpose, types, order of dependencies, and the location of the dependent services or building blocks. With the dependency description, it is obvious whether two mechanisms in the same protocol graph must run in a sequence, can run in parallel, or they are mutually exclusive.

Dependency can be a requirement from a building block. For example, a building block which implements a prioritization algorithm can be dependent on authentication and authorization building blocks. Authentication and authorization is required to be executed before prioritization. Requirement and ordering represents the purpose of a dependency.

The types of dependency can be hard or soft. In the case of a hard dependency, the dependency requirement must be fulfilled and a service or a building block can not perform its task without having that dependency fulfilled. Soft dependencies are the best practices for optimization. For example, the dependency between the compression service and the encryption service is a soft dependency requirement. Compression needs to be done before encryption. Performance deficits happen when encryption is done before Compression.

The order of dependent components (building blocks or services) needs to be considered during composition. Unordered components can be executed in any order or in parallel manner. For example, flow control and error control services can run in parallel. Two services or building blocks are mutually exclusive when they can not run in parallel in the same protocol graph. For example, no two different compression mechanisms can be used simultaneously for compressing the same data. Compression building blocks are mutually exclusive. A sequence of functionalities is required when an effect must be provided before another one. For instance, the error detection must be done before the error correction.

The location of the dependent building blocks or services is essential to describe. The dependent building blocks or services can be available on the local node, on the middle boxes (for example, routers or switches), or on the end point. Specifying the location of the dependent building blocks or services will relieve the composition engine from searching, which can save composition time.

The less dependency a building block has, the easier it is to reuse. Moreover, not every building block has dependency. Therefore, the dependency description is optional and can be used optionally in a service selection and composition process.

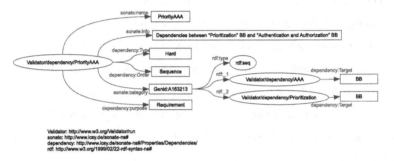

Fig. 3.6 Description of dependencies between prioritization BB and authentication and authorization BB

3.3.10 Types

An application developer might specify requirements as mandatory or optional. Suitable services are obtained by using mandatory effects. Optional effects can be used to select the best service when there is more than one suitable service.

3.3.11 Aggregators

Aggregators are used as a predicate with the effect to create a new effect. Aggregators are necessary to compare between the requirements and the offerings. For example, MTU, Aggregated Delay, and Average Throughput. Aggregators also specify an interval which is the range between an upper bound and a lower bound. An example of a requirement is $\{(Delay >= 50ms)AND(Delay <= 100ms)\}$ which means that the delay must be between 50 ms and 100 ms. Aggregators also specify rating and scaling. Scaling takes two values and checks whether a value is within that scale. Rating takes one value for ratings based on the given scale.

3.3.12 Description of Dependencies

Dependencies can occur between two services, two building blocks, and between a service and a building block. Based on these dependency patterns, three scenarios have been constructed.

1. *Dependency between services*

   An example of this dependency is "error detection before error correction" where error detection provides only an error indication service and error correction offers only an error removal service. This dependency is hard because the error correction can not provide its service without getting indications from error detection. Figure 3.5 shows the description of this dependency.

2. *Dependency between building blocks*

   A dependency can arise between building blocks as shown in the Figure 3.6. In this example, a building block which implements a priority level requires a building block which implements authentication and authorization. The first building block can be executed only when positive feedback comes from the second building block which is a definition of sequence, meaning that the second building block must be executed before the first building block. Here, the dependency is not only for ordering (as in the case of first scenario) but also for requirement. The dependency is hard because without fulfilling this dependency, a priority cannot be provided.

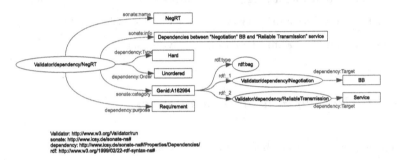

Fig. 3.7 Description of dependencies between negotiation BB and reliable transmission service

3. *Dependency between a building block and a service*

   Dependencies can also happen between a building block and a service as shown in Figure 3.7. In this example, a building block which implements a negotiation mechanism requires a reliable transmission service. This is a definition of a requirement because the building block requires the service for performing its task. The dependency is hard as the dependency must be fulfilled.

3.3.13 Description of a Communication Service

The description of an RTT estimation service is shown in Figure 3.8. In the Figure, the blue text represents "which" nodes are related and the red text represents "how / through which" they are related. For example, RTTEstimator has an effect PayloadPassthrough. Here, "RTTEstimator" and "PayloadPassthrough" nodes are related and their relation is made through "effect". The green arrow is read as "has". There are two namespaces used in the Figure: sonate and rdf. They are used to identify each node uniquely. Even though sonate namespace is used here, however, the langauge is not sonate specific.

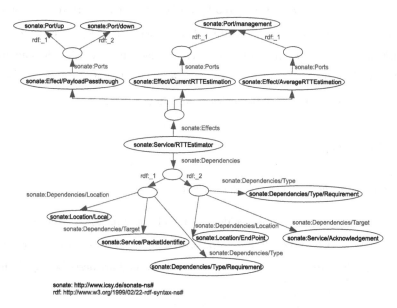

Fig. 3.8 The description of an RTT estimation service

The service is represented by the effects offered by the underlying building block. The building block offers three effects through its ports. These effects are: *PayloadPassthrough* (i.e., does not change the contents of a packet), *CurrentRTTEsitmation* (estimates RTT by measuring a single packet), and *AverageRTTEstimation* (estimates RTT by measuring some packets). Different building blocks might implement different strategies for calculating AverageRTT and CurrentRTT. For achieving flexibility, the implementation should not influence on the description. The description needs to provide interfaces for a certain effect. The application needs to know only the interfaces not the implementation details. For example, the up and down interfaces offer the *PayloadPassthrough* effect. *CurrentRTTEstimation* and *AverageRTTEstimation* are offered by the management interface. For using the *RTTEstimator* service, certain other services such as *PacketIdentifier* and *Acknowledgment* are required which are described by using dependencies. The *PacketIdentifier* service is locally available but the *Acknowledgment* service is only available at the EndPoint.

3.3.13.1 Grammar

The rules of the language are described as below

1. Service selection requires the description of the application requirements, the network and the administrator constraints, and the network offerings. All of these requirements, constraints and offerings are described by using the following construct

$$\{effect\ operator\ attribute\}$$

An effect is a single outcome of an execution of algorithms or protocols represented as building blocks or protocol graphs. Therefore, an application defines its requirement by using effects. An attribute is a value of an effect. For example, 0% is an attribute of the effect packet loss.

An operator connects an effect to an attribute. The packet loss offered by a retransmission building block is written as

$$\{LossRatio = 0\%\}$$

This simple construct is used to express the requirements of an application. For example, the error correction demand of an email application is expressed as

$$\{ErrorCorrection = True\}$$

This construct allows the description of the network offerings. For example, the packet loss offering of a retransmission algorithm is expressed as

$$\{LossRatio = 0\%\}$$

A network or administrator constraints can be expressed by using the construct. For example, for using a certain network, authentication must be performed

$$\{Authentication = True\}$$

2. The usage of an effect in the description is mandatory. But, the usage of an operator and an attribute is optional. For example, the error correction demand can be described as

$$\{ErrorCorrection\}$$

3. Every description of application requirements, and network offerings must contain one or more $\{effect\ operator\ attribute\}$ construct.

4. The description of administrator policies and network constraints must also use the same construct. However, they might not be present in the description as there may be no administrator policies or network constraints.

5. Dependency description in the offerings is optional. This requires the information about the availability of other services.

6. Linear prioritization of effects is assigned using the construct $\{effect\ operator\ attribute\}$ as well. For example, the prioritization of end-to-end delay, loss ratio and usage cost are assigned as

$$\{EndToEndDelay = 0.5\}, \{PktLossRatio = 0.4\}, \{UsageCost = 0.1\}$$

7. Pairwise prioritization of effects is assigned using the construct $\{(effect1, effect2)\ operator\ attribute\}$. For example, the pairwise prioritization between end-to-end delay and loss ratio can be expressed as

$$\{(EndToEndDelay, PktLossRatio) = 9\}$$

8. Each optional (non-functional) effect is associated with a specific mathematical operator. For example, the effect ProcessingDelay uses the $+$ operator.

The construct $\{effect\ operator\ attribute\}$ supports to describe both fine-grained and coarse-grained functionalities in a similar way. For example, the

ProcessingTime of a building block or a protocol graph can be expressed by using the same construct.

3.4 Fulfilling Language Requirements By CSDL

The requirements for the proposed language have been discussed in Section 3.2.3. Based on the requirements, a communication service description language has been proposed in Section 3.3. In this section, it is discussed how both the mandatory and optional requirements in Section 3.2.3 can be fulfilled by the proposed language.

3.4.1 Fulfilling Mandatory Requirements

The proposed language fulfills all of the mandatory requirements as described below:

Modularity: The language is able to describe all of the components of selection and composition including application and user requirements, network properties, administrator policies, network and hardware constraints in a modular basis. Since all of the components are described by using the same construct *(effect operator attribute)*, they can be described in a parallel manner. Moreover, whenever the value of $effect$, $operator$, or $attribute$ of one component changes, it does not affect the description of other components.

Information hiding: The language is capable of hiding implementation details of a building block or a protocol graph as it describes only the resultant outcome of a building block or a protocol graph by using the construct *(effect operator attribute)* where the effects are pre-defined in taxonomies.

The language does not describe the internal implementation mechanisms (a method, or an operation) of a building block or a protocol graph. Therefore, an user (or an application) can request for the result that he needs, not the method which produces that result.

Predecessor/successor knowledge: During service composition, dependencies are considered to prepare a fully functional service. These dependencies can be between building blocks, between services, and, between a building block and a service. The proposed language gives the possibility to describe dependencies of a building block which requires the knowledge of its predecessor and successor. Dependency description can increase efficiency as it deducts searching and matching time. However, it reduces flexibility and re-usability. To solve the problem, the dependency description is kept optional. As the proposed language considered dependency description as optional, no predecessor or successor knowledge is required to describe a building block or a protocol graph.

Description of different types of communication functionalities: The functional effects of Figure 3.3 show that the proposed language can describe not only the functionalities of the higher layer protocols but also the lower layer protocols. As the taxonomy is extensible with new effects, future communication protocols can be described.

No dependency exists with composition approaches: Composition approaches differ in terms of the time of composition: design time, deployment time, or runtime. The language has the following components: effects, influence, interface, datatype, dependencies, operators, types, aggregators, and units. None of these components is specific to any composition approach. Therefore, both existing and new composition approaches can use the language.

Selection and composition of building blocks: The language supports selection and composition of building blocks to produce a protocol graph for communication association. Composition approaches can determine ordering of functionalities during 1. design time such as template-based composition or 2. during runtime. In the first case, dependency description of building blocks is defined by the designer. In the second case, the optional dependency description component of the language is required which reduces flexibility and re-usability. When the ordering of building block is determined as in the first case, the next step is to select a suitable (or the most suitable) building block. As the language describes both the requirements and offerings of a building block by using the syntax *(effect operator attribute)*, suitable building blocks can be selected by matching their requirements and offerings as described in Section 4.1. The most suitable building block for composition is selected by using a multi-criteria decision analysis method as discussed in Section 4.2.

Extensible: The proposed language can be extended with new vocabularies and grammars to fulfill the demands of the future. Both the functional effects of Figure 3.3 and non functional effects of Figure 3.4 can be extended with new vocabularies. The grammar in Section 3.3.13.1 can also be extended.

Independence of selection and composition mechanisms: The language has no dependency with the selection and composition mechanisms (such as multi-criteria decision analysis methods, and template-based or other composition approaches) who use it. Therefore, both existing, and new selection and composition methods can use the language. In addition, the language itself can be extended with updated vocabularies and grammars.

Can describe different types of application requirements: The language is capable of describing different types of application requirements. The "Effect", "Operator", "Attribute", and "Types" components of the language are used to do this task. Using the construct *(effect operator attribute)*, both functional and non-functional effects are specified. In addition, several requirements are aggregated by using the mathematical or logical operators. By using the component "Type", both mandatory and optional requirements are specified.

Aggregation of end-to-end properties: The language is able to aggregate end-to-end properties of different networks. These properties are specified by the non-functional effects as shown in Figure 3.4. To aggregate the properties, mathematical operators are used. With the language, it is also possible to specify mathematical equations to accomplish customized computation such as average, minimum, maximum, and aggregated.

Capable of describing dependency: The language is able to describe dependency while ensuring flexibility. To achieve that, the dependency description is declared as optional in the language. Therefore, whenever efficiency is more important than flexibility, then dependency description can be used. Section 3.3.12 shows the dependency description between services, building blocks, and, a building block and a service.

Able to describe augmented effects: In a selection and composition approach such as NENA and SONATE, a building block augments effects. This augmented effect is described in the language as non-functional effects. Moreover, the language provides a list of operator and each non-functional effect is associated with an operator. Operators might be assigned by a service broker. However, as an application requirement, application developers are allowed to change the operator for each non-functional effect.

Independent from the granularity of building blocks: The language is not dependent on the granularity of building blocks and is able to describe their capabilities using the same construct *(effect operator attribute)*.

Capable of describing the service independent on their location: The language is able to describe services of building blocks and protocol graphs independent on their location of residence including end-nodes, and middle-boxes. No component of the language is tightly coupled to their residence.

Independent from Application Programming Interface (API): The language is not constructed considering any particular APIs, therefore, not tightly coupled to any APIs. As the language uses commonly used vocabularies and generic syntax, future APIs should be able to use the language.

Supports aggregation of BB effects: By composing building blocks, protocol graphs are constructed. The effects of a protocol graph are the aggregated effects of the composed building blocks. As all of the building blocks are described using the syntax *(effect operator attribute)*, they can be aggregated easily. Functional effects are aggregated by listing the *(effect operator attribute)*. Non-functional effects are aggregated by listing the *(effect operator attribute)*. The aggregated attribute for each non-functional effect is computed by a specific mathematical operator, may be assigned by the broker. Therefore, the language supports aggregation of BB effects.

Description of a protocol graph: The language is able to describe a protocol graph which is the output of a composition method. The protocol graph description consists of a unique identifier, mandatory (functional) and optional (non-functional) effects as offerings, and the connections between the interfaces of different building blocks. The component "ID" of the language is used to identify a protocol graph. The "Type" component of the language as well as the construct *(effect operator attribute)* are used to describe functional and non-functional effects. The connection between the interfaces of different building blocks is described by the component "connection". The description of a protocol graph is shown in Appendix A.5.

Description of building blocks: The language is capable of describing building blocks. Each building block has a unique identifier, one or more interfaces, the data types for the interfaces, and the effects that are provided by them. The component "ID" of the language is used to identify a building block. The components "Port", "DataType", "Type", and the construct (effect operator attribute) are used to describe the remaining part.

One language for all components: Using the same language, all of the components of selection (and composition) including application requirements, administration constraints, network constraints, building blocks, and protocol graph can be described. Using the same vocabularies (functional and non-functional effects) and grammars *(effect operator attribute)* made it feasible.

3.4.2 Fulfilling Optional Requirements

The proposed language fulfills all of the optional requirements as described below:

Creation of a protocol graph from an existing one: Using the language, it is possible to make a new protocol graph by modifying the description of an existing protocol graph. As protocol graphs are described using XML, they can be modified easily.

Usability of the language: The proposed language is usable in terms of the criteria specified by Jakob Nielson [85]. The language is "easy to learn" and "easy to remember" as it deduced to a simple construct *(effect operator attribute)* and pre-defined vocabularies (the terms that are commonly used by network researchers). As all components of selection and composition are described by using the same language, only one time learning is necessary. As the language has been developed by using XML-Schema, "few errors", "efficient to use", and "subjectively pleasing" can be expected assuming that the user knows the XML-Schema already.

Selection of the most appropriate protocol graph: Section 4.2 describes how the proposed language assists in selecting the most appropriate protocol graph.

Supports rating of effects: The language supports rating of services between building blocks / protocol graphs as it can express parameters for rating using the construct *(effect operator attribute)*.

Independent from objective function: The language is not dependent on any objective function, that is used to rate between services of building blocks / protocol graphs. As the required parameters for rating is also expressed using the same construct *(effect operator attribute)* as describing application requirements and network offerings, any objective function may use the language.

Assists in transparent selection and composition: The language supports transparent selection and composition of building blocks. Section 4.2 provides an automatic selection approach where the best protocol graph is selected automatically based on application requirements. In this case, users/application developers are not aware of the complexity of the selection. For a composition approach including the template-based approach, automatic selection of building blocks is necessary to create a protocol graph.

Keeping the selection automatic, the language hides the complexity of selection and composition.

Supports verification and validation: The language supports syntactic verification and validation mechanisms and is not dependent on those mechanisms. The result of the verification and validation mechanism is expressed as non-functional effects and is expressed by the construct *(effect operator attribute)*. Using the same construct, the requirements of the application for the mechanism can also be expressed. Therefore, the broker can check whether a composed protocol graph is valid just by matching the requirements and the offerings.

Supports heterogeneity: The language is able to describe the capabilities of the mechanisms that are necessary for supporting heterogeneity using the construct *(effect operator attribute)*. As the language is extensible with new vocabularies and grammars, the effects from the building blocks representing future negotiation algorithms can also be described.

3.5 Validation of CSDL

The aim of this section is to validate the description language by describing the effects of currently the most used transport layer protocol, the Transmission Control Protocol (TCP) [30]. Sequencing building blocks for constituting a protocol graph is the main task of a composition algorithm such as the template-based composition approach. The target of this validation is not to show how a composition is done, rather to show whether the proposed language can describe the effects of the protocol, TCP.

The list of the functional effects that are offered by TCP protocol are *Stream, FullDuplex, ConnectionMgmt, InOrderDelivery, DuplicateControl,*

ErrorDetection, LossDetection, ErrorControl, EndToEndFlowControl, Con-gestionControl. Given that the functional effect of each building block is described by the construct *(effect operator attribute)*, the list is obtained by using the Algorithm 1.

Data: integer totalBB such that totalBB $>= 0$;
         string[][][] effectsOfEachBB;
Result: functionalEffects;
          nonfunctionalEffects;
string[] functionalEffects = null;

string[] nonfunctionalEffects = null;

int functionalIndex = 0;

int nonfunctionalIndex = 0;

for *(int i = totalBB; i >= 1; i = i - 1)* **do**

    for *(int j = effectsOfEachBB[i].Size; j >= 1; j = j - 1)* **do**

        if *(IsFunctional(effectsOfEachBB[i][j][0], Functional) = true*
        then

            if *(StringMatch(effectsOfEachBB[i][j][1], functionalEffects)*
            = false **then**

                functionalEffects[functionalIndex] =
                effectsOfEachBB[i][j][1];

                functionalIndex = functionalIndex + 1;

            end

        else

            if *(StringMatch(effectsOfEachBB[i][j][1],*

            nonfunctionalEffects) = false **then**

                nonfunctionalEffects[nonfunctionalIndex] =

                effectsOfEachBB[i][j][1];

                nonfunctionalIndex = nonfunctionalIndex + 1;

            end

        end

    end

end

return functionalEffects, nonfunctionalEffects;

Algorithm 1 computeEffects (string[][][] effectsOfEachBB, int totalBB)

TCP transmits the *Stream* type data in a *FullDuplex* mode. It uses the mechanism "three-way hand shake" to offer the effect *ConnectionMgmt*. Moreover, it utilizes sequence numbers to provide the effects *InOrderDelivery* and *DuplicateControl*. The protocol offers the effect *ErrorDetection* by using the checksum mechanism. Moreover, it provides the *EndToEndFlowControl* effect by using one of the sliding window protocols such as Go-Back-N, and selective repeat. Moreover, TCP applies acknowledgement mechanisms including cumulative and selective, and retransmission mechanisms such as Go-Back-N, and selective repeat to provide the effects *LossDetection* and *ErrorControl*. The *CongestionControl* effect is provided by the TCP protocol using one of the mechanisms; slow start, congestion avoidance, fast retransmit, and fast recovery [8].

Data: integer totalBB such that totalBB >= 0;
       string[] nonfunctionalEffects;
       string[][][] effectsOfEachBB;
       int index = 0;
Result: aggregatedValueEffects;
double[] aggregatedValueEffects = null;

operator math;

for *(int i = 0; i <= nonfunctionalEffects.Size; i = i + 1)* **do**

    double aggregatedValueEffect = 0;

    math = mathOpForEffect(nonfunctionalEffects[i]);

    for *(int j = totalBB; j >= 1; j = j - 1)* **do**

        for *(int k = effectsOfEachBB[j].Size; k >= 1; k = k - 1)* **do**

            if *(StringMatch(nonfunctionalEffects[i],*

            effectsOfEachBB[j][k][1]) = true **then**

                aggregatedValueEffect = math (aggregatedValueEffect,

                effectsOfEachBB[j][k][3]);

            end

        end

    end

    aggregatedValueEffects[i] = aggregatedValueEffect;

end

return aggregatedValueEffects;

Algorithm 2 computeEffects (string[][][] effectsOfEachBB, string[] nonfunctionalEffects, int totalBB)

Some of the non-functional effects that may be offered by the TCP protocol graph are *ConnectionMgmt.SetUpDelay, PktLossRatio*. As TCP uses three-way hand shake, its *SetUpDelay* is lower than the SCTP protocol [119] which uses four-way hand shake. The value of the effect *PktLossRatio* could be used to choose an appropriate retransmission mechanism. TCP could also offer other non-functional effects including ProcessingDelay, MemoryUsage, and CPUUsage whose values are specific to a particular OS, Memory, and CPU. Given that the non-functional effect of each building block is described by the construct *(effect operator attribute)*, the list is obtained by using the Algorithm 1. Moreover, the value of each non-functional effect is aggregated by using the Algorithm 2.

Selection of Suitable TCP

An application that wants to retrieve functionalities from the network like TCP protocol (for example, SSH, telnet, SMTP) specifies two types of requirements: Mandatory and Optional.

Mandatory = (Stream, FullDuplex, ConnectionMgmt, InOrderDelivery, DuplicateControl, ErrorDetection, LossDetection, ErrorControl, EndToEndFlowControl, CongestionControl)

Optional = (ConnectionMgmt.SetUpDelay, ProcessingDelay, MemoryUsage, CPUUsage)

A protocol graph is a suitable TCP if it's functional effects fully matches with the mandatory application requirements.

Selection of the Best TCP

When functional effects of a protocol graph match with the mandatory application requirements, it is suitable to use by the application. However, mandatory application requirements may be fulfilled by several protocol graphs. In that case, the best protocol graph is chosen by using the optional requirements specified by the application. Each non-functional effect that is offered by a protocol graph has an associated value. These values may differ in suitable protocol graphs. As an example, the value *ConnectionMgmt.SetUpDelay* for TCP protocol is not the same as SCTP protocol since the former one uses three-way handshake and the last one uses four-way handshake. In this thesis (described in the next chapter), the

Analytic Hierarchy Process (AHP) has been adapted to select the best protocol graph which uses optional application requirements and non-functional
offering of protocol graphs.

Combined Effects of a Protocol Graph

Two algorithms, one for listing both the functional and non-functional
effects and another for retrieving the value of the effects, are used to compute
the combined effects of a protocol graph.

The combined functional effects are listed sequentially from bottom to
top using Algorithm 1 where *totalBB* is the total number of building blocks
in a protocol graph and *functionalEffects* and *nonfunctionalEffects* are string
arrays which store all of the functional and non-functional effects of a protocol graph respectively. The *effectsOfEachBB* is an array where the effects of
each building block are stored in a pattern *[type, effect, operator, attribute]*.
If a protocol graph has 5 BBs, then the value of totalBB is 5 and the value
of effectsOfEachBB is all of the effects of the building block 5. The function
IsFunctional checks whether an effect is Functional or Non-functional. Two
StringMatch functions are used in the Algorithm 1, to compare the name
of effect with the already constructed list (functionalEffects, nonfunctional-
Effects) to avoid duplicate entry in the aggregated effect lists.

Non-functional effects	Operators for aggregation
Compression.Speed	+
Compression.Ratio	max (considering the best case)
Compression.Loss	+
Decompression.Speed	+
Addressing.Space	max (considering the best case)
Security.KeyStrength	min (considering the worst case)
Bandwidth	+
Goodput	+
SuccessRate	+
PktErrorProbability	+
PktLossRatio	+
PktLossProbability	+
QueingDelay	+
PropagationDelay	+
TransmissionDelay	+
ProcessingDelay	+
MemoryUsage	+
CPUUsage	+
EnergySaving.Consumption	+
ConnectionMgmt.SetUpDelay	+
Jitter	+
Throughput	+
DataLoss	+

Table 3.3 Operators to aggregate non-functional effects

Using Algorithm 1, the non-functional effects are listed in the nonfunctionalEffects array. For each non-functional effect, the combined value of a protocol graph is computed sequentially from bottom to top using Algorithm 2. The following algorithm takes effects (effectsOfEachBB), nonfunctional effects (nonfunctionalEffects), and the total number of building blocks as input and computes the aggregated value for non-functional effects for a complete protocol graph. For computing the value of a non-functional effect, math (mathematical operators such as $+, min, max$) is used. Each non-functional effect is associated with a specific math operator such as ProcessingDelay uses the $+$ operator. The function mathOpForEffect returns the mathematical operator for a particular effect. A suggestion for operators for non-functional effects is shown in Table 3.3 which may be stored in the knowledge base of the broker. Most of the non-functional effects except Compression.Ratio, Addressing.Space, and Security.KeyStrength can be aggregated using the + operator. For the effects Compression.Ratio and Addressing.Space, the best case is considered whereas for the effect Security.KeyStrength, the worst case is considered as security effects impacts more (in terms of damaging a network) than other effects. When several building blocks providing compression functionality are used in a protocol graph, the value of their non-functional effect Compression.Ratio is the maximum of the values provided by those building blocks. Similarly, when several building blocks providing addressing functionality are aggregated, the value of their non-functional effect Addressing.Space is the maximum of the values provided by those building blocks. However, when several building blocks providing security functionality are aggregated, the value of their non-functional effect Security.KeyStrength is the minimum of the values provided by those building blocks. Instead of using min, max operators, other solution would be to list the non-functional effects one after another (similar to functional effects) that are provided by several building blocks (for example, $Addressing = 32, Addressing = 128$). The disadvantage with this approach is that internal details (how many building blocks provide the same non-functional effects) are exposed which is the violation of the optional language property "assists in transparent selection and composition". The advantage with this approach is that selection (and composition) mechanisms is flexible to choose one of them as non-functional effects.

The parameters totalBB is the total number of building blocks in a protocol graph. The aggregatedValueEffects array returns the value of all of the non-functional effects of a protocol graph. For example, if the name of a non-functional effect is "ProcessingDelay" and the value of the totalBB

is 5, then aggregatedValueEffect returns the aggregated value of ProcessingDelay of all of the 5 building blocks. The aggregated value of each effect
is then stored in the aggregatedValueEffects array.

4 Service Selection

Using different selection and composition approaches in the same architecture such as SONATE, the possibility of offering many similar coarse-grained services (e.g., protocol graphs) with different qualities of service is increasing. Such a case can be even higher when many different future network architectural approaches (e.g., NENA, RBA, RNA) co-exist. Correspondingly, similar services with different qualities of service can also be provided by many fine-grained functionalities (e.g., building blocks). Therefore, it will be required to select a suitable (discussed in Section 4.1), or the best service (described in Section 4.2), from alternative services. This chapter proposes a matching process and an adapted analytic hierarchy process. The matching process is used to select suitable services based on application requirements. When more than one suitable service is available, the adapted analytic hierarchy process is used to select the best service.

4.1 Selection of Suitable Services

When a functionality, or a set of functionalities, fulfills all of the mandatory
application requirements, the service of that functionality is suitable to be
used by the application. The related work of selecting suitable services is
presented at first in Section 4.1.1. After that, a matching process is proposed
to select suitable services in Section 4.1.2.

4.1.1 Related Work

In [75] and [133], the authors choose suitable netlets (i.e., composed protocol
stacks) by filtering based on user/application requirements and system policies. Only the netlets which succeeded filtration are used. For example, an
application requires that the data should be encrypted. The netlets which
offer this functionality are used later on to select the optimal one. However,
they did not mention which mechanism is used for filtering.

In [96] and [97], suitable services are selected by comparing the requirements and offerings of inherent properties. An offer is said to be suitable if
the URIs of the offering is the same as the URI of the requirements. If a
property is also described by parameters, the boundaries of parameters of
the offering must also fit to the request.

Selection of micro-protocols is required during the protocol composition
of the configurable high level protocols approach [17]. This is an event driven
approach where each micro-protocol consists of a set of its own private
events, some imported and exported events. Each event is handled by one
or more event handlers, which invokes one or more micro-protocols in a
certain order. Thereby, each event makes a partial composition of protocol

graph. The size and the structure of the protocol graph depends on the sequence of the events generated and handled.

In this approach, the selection of micro-protocols for a certain event is static as it is predetermined how that event is treated by the handler. Changing of a selection, or even of a composition (i.e., event handler in this case) mechanism requires to change in the handler. However, this approach does not provide a generic mechanism for selecting suitable micro-protocols or the best micro-protocol.

In the adaptive (a dynamically assemble protocol transformation, integration and validation environment) system, the final session configuration (discussed in 3.1) is sent to the component called Transport Kernel Object (TKO) which selects suitable mechanisms from the TKO class library [102]. However, how the selection is done is not mentioned by the authors.

4.1.2 Suitable Services Selection Method

An application requirement is specified by using two types of effects: mandatory and optional. Similarly, offered services are also described using those two types of effects.

Suitable services are chosen by matching the mandatory effects of an application requirement with the mandatory effects (functional) of the offering. For example, an application specifies InOrderDelivery, DuplicateControl, ErrorDetection, LossDetection and ErrorCorrection as mandatory requirements. When the mandatory effects of a protocol graph matches with this requirement, the broker selects that protocol graph as a suitable service.

For matching the application requirements with the network offerings, each effect must be uniquely identified. This necessitates developing a taxonomy of effects to describe communication services as shown in Figures 3.3 and 3.4. The earlier version of the taxonomy was published in [66]. This taxonomy facilitates an application developer to specify effects either in a generic manner or in a specific way. For example, an application developer can ask for the "Security" effect in general, $\{Security = True\}$, or it can ask for the "DataOriginAuthentication" effect, $\{DataOriginAuthentication = True\}$, to be more precise.

4.2 Selection of the Best Service

During the selection process, several of them can be determined as suitable services when they match the mandatory requirements from the application. In that case, the best service should be selected and used. In this chapter, the Analytic Hierarchy Process (AHP) is adapted by several mapping mechanisms to select the best service automatically.

4.2.1 Related Work

For making managerial decisions, multi-criteria decision analysis (MCDA) methods are used. There are many MCDA approaches. The following MCDA methods are considered in this thesis:

1. MAUT: In the Multi-attribute Utility Theory (MAUT) [64], a utility function is constructed for each criteria (attribute). An example of a utility function is that decreasing loss rate increases the utility in a network. A candidate alternative can have many criteria. An aggregate function is used to aggregate the utility of all of the criteria for a candidate alternative. The alternative with the highest value is selected as the best one.

2. AHP: The Analytic Hierarchy Process (AHP) [100] was invented by Thomas Lorie Saaty. In AHP, a set of criteria is selected to achieve a goal, for instance, selecting the best service. Pairwise priority is then assigned among the criteria and among the candidate alternatives for each criteria. After that, the overall priority is calculated. The alternative with the highest priority is selected as the best one. In AHP, it is possible to check the consistency of the evaluation measures. The pairwise priority

value can be changed in the case of inconsistency. Moreover, it supports inter-dependencies among different criteria.

3. Evamix: Henk Voogd proposed the Evaluation matrix (Evamix) [136] method. In Evamix qualitative and quantitative criteria (also called ordinal and nominal criteria) are selected. Then, the dominance scores and the standardized dominance scores (in the same measurement unit) of all qualitative and quantitative criteria are calculated. After that, the overall dominance score is calculated. Then, appraisal scores are calculated. The alternative with the highest appraisal score is selected.

4. Regime: Regime was proposed by Hinloopen [55]. Since regime supports mixed data, both cardinal (quantitative) and ordinal (qualitative) criterion can be included.

5. ELECTRE III: Electre III was developed by Roy [99]. Electre supports only cardinal ranking, whereas Regime supports both cardinal and ordinal ranking.

6. NAIADE: Giuseppe Munda developed a novel approach to imprecise assessment and decision environment (NAIADE) [83]. The process of NAIDE is in a sequence: the alternatives are pairwise compared, all qualitative and quantitative criteria are aggregated, then the alternatives are evaluated.

7. MOP/GP: The basis of Multi-Objective-Programming (MOP), Goal Programming (GP) and their variants are mathematical models [34]. Rather than ranking a finite number of alternatives, MOP/GP generates alternatives based on mathematical model.

   In MOP/GP, a set of Pareto efficient solution are identified. Then, the most preferred solution is identified together with the decision maker.

Lars Völker et. al. [133] used MAUT for selecting the optimal one from a set of alternative candidates so called "Netlets" at runtime based on user requirements.

This work is based on a clean slate network architecture approach called Netlet-based Node Architecture (NENA) [1] where each node consists of a set of netlets and each netlet is made of a set of building blocks composed by using the netlet editor at design time.

Based on the application requirements, they filtered a set of suitable netlets which are considered later on for obtaining the optimal one using MAUT.

For getting the best alternative using MAUT, the utility value of each alternative $v(a_i)$ is computed using the formula

$$v(a_i) = \sum_{j=1}^{m} w_j * v_j(c_j(a_i)) \tag{4.1}$$

where alternatives and criteria are denoted by $(a_i \ where \ i = 1,..,n)$ and $(c_j \ where \ j = 1,..,m)$ respectively. w_j and v_j represent the weight and value functions for each criterion.

Then, the alternatives are sorted in descending order based on their calculated utility value. The alternative with the highest value is selected as the best one.

This approach is simple and requires users or application developers to assign weight for each criterion. However, assigning a relative weight among the criteria is easier for the users than assigning an absolute weight for each criterion which is not considered in this approach. Moreover, this approach does not support an interdependence among the criteria which is seen in communication services. In addition, this method requires input value functions $v_j(c_j(a_i))$ for each criteria which should be given beforehand or must be passed during calculating the overall value of each alternative. The value functions vary from criterion to criterion. For example, the value function of the criteria "Latency" is different from the value function of the criteria "Effective Bitstrength"[134]. This method assumes that users always assign consistent weight to the criteria which is usually not the case. The authors of the paper [134] mentioned the advantage of Analytic Hierarchy Process(AHP) over MAUT as it does consistency checking.

Qualitative properties of B. Reuther et. al. assist in selecting the optimal service [96][97]. The quality of an offering can be expressed as

$$Pq_i = \sum_{i=1}^{n} w_i q_{i,k} \qquad (4.2)$$

where the weight, $w_i \in [0,1] \subset \Re$, is the relative ratings of properties which is specified in the requirements and is determined by the application developers. Relative rating of the offered TSPs for each property is calculated based on the subjective or objective methods and is specified as $q_{i,k} \in [0,1] \subset \Re$. Then the TSPs are sorted in descending order according to their value of Pq_i. The TSP with the topmost quality value is selected as the best TSP as long as that TSP can be accessed otherwise the next TSP is selected. To determine the quality of an offering $q_{i,k}$, either the subjective or the objective method is used. In the subjective method, $q_{i,k}$ is defined by an expert such as an application developer. The objective method is based on a benchmark Q_i and a rating function f_r. The rating function grades the result of a benchmark which is predefined and can be adapted by the experts such as application developer. Experts can define their own rating function. The author proposed to use a fixed function $f_r(x) = h_{a,b,y}(g(x, lb, ub))$ where $g(x, lb, ub)$ and $h_{a,b,y}$ are linear and non-linear mapping respectively.

The function $g(x, lb, ub)$ is expressed as

$$g(x, lb, ub) = \begin{cases} 0 & \text{if } (x < lb \wedge lb < ub) \vee (x > lb \wedge lb > ub) \\ \frac{x-lb}{ub-lb} & \text{if } x \in [lb, ub] \\ 1 & \text{if } (x > ub \wedge ub > lb) \vee (x < ub \wedge ub < lb) \end{cases}$$

(4.3)

which is used to rate linearly the offered values to a $[0,1]$ scale. For providing non-linearity to the values obtained from $g(x, lb, ub)$, $h_{a,b,y}$ is used which is expressed as

$$h_{a,b,y}(x) = \begin{cases} (1 - (1 - \frac{x}{a})^y)b & \text{if } 0 \leq x < a \\ b & \text{if } x = a \\ (\frac{x-a}{1-a})^y(1-b)+b & \text{if } a < x \leq 1 \end{cases}$$
$$where \ x \in [0,1], \ y \in \Re^+, \ a, b \in]0, 1[\vee a, b = 0 \vee a, b = 1$$

(4.4)

[97] uses an example to illustrate how parameters for the function $h_{a,b,y}(x)$ could be determined. According to the example, for determining quality for a particular property, this approach requires the following parameters to be specified $pq_i = \{URI, q, lb, ub, a, b, y\}$. For example, an application requirement for the qualitative property delay is as follows: $pq_i = \{http : //www.icsy.de/inherent/properties/delay, f(50) = 0.5, 200, 10, 0, 0, y\}$. Then, the linear function calculates $g(50, 200, 10)$ as

$$g(50, 200, 10) = \frac{x - lb}{lb - ub} = \frac{50 - 200}{10 - 200} \approx 0.79$$

Which means that $h(0.79, y, 0, 0) = 0.5$ provides $y = \frac{log 0.5}{log 0.79} \approx 2.94$. For details, please take a look at [97].

The above mentioned rating functions work well as long as only one hint for a particular property is specified. However, this approach cannot provide optimal solution if more than one hints are provided. In this case, only an approximation is possible.

In the following section, a Multi-Criteria Decision Analysis (MCDA) method namely the Analytic Hierarchy Process (AHP) [100] has been adapted to select the best service automatically. The earlier version of the method has been presented in the ITU Kleidoscope conference [66]. The matured version of the method has been nominated by ITU as a standardization candidate [4].

4.2.2 Best Service Selection Method

Selecting the best service using a single selection criterion is trivial. For example, if there are two communication services where one offers 100ms end-to-end delay and another offers 200 ms, then obviously the one with less delay should be selected.

However, communication services have multiple selection criteria such as delay, throughput, loss ratio, jitter and cost. Therefore, selecting the best communication service is a Multi-Criteria Decision Making problem (MCDM). For solving such a problem, several Multi-Criteria Decision Analysis (MCDA) approaches are used in managerial science such as Analytic Hierarchy Process (AHP), ELECTREIII [99], Evamix [136], Multiple Attribute Utility Theory (MAUT) [64], Multi-Objective-Programming (MOP), Goal Programming (GP) [34], NAIADE [83] and Regime [55].

The AHP, to select the best service, is chosen for several reasons, firstly, it uses an absolute scale to derive priorities, secondly, it uses pairwise priority assignment, thirdly, there is a way to check the consistency of the evaluation measures.

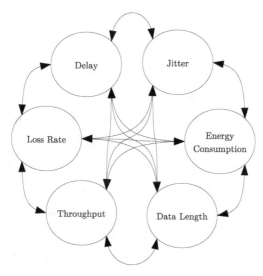

Fig. 4.1 Dependencies among Criteria

4.2.2.1 Interdependence of Selection Criteria

Selection criteria are dependent on each other as shown in Figure 4.1. But, how the criteria are interdependent depends upon the mechanism (TCP or UDP) being used.

Delay is dependent on loss rate, jitter, throughput, data length and energy consumption. In this section, all of the examples consider using transmission control protocol (TCP). Delay increases with loss rate because packets need to be retransmitted in case of loss. Delay increases with jitter as packets might arrive in different orders, in case of jitter. The reordering of those packets increases the delay. Delay decreases with throughput. Delay increases with data length as longer packets might need to wait in the queue. Energy consumption is increased with delay as keeping the packet in the queue requires energy.

Similarly, loss rate is dependent on delay, throughput, jitter, energy consumption and data length. Loss rate increases with delay as packets not acknowledged within a timing threshold are assumed to have been lost. Loss rate decreases as throughput increases. Loss rate can also be influenced by jitter. Loss rate can be increased with increasing jitter. Loss rate increases energy consumption as resending lost packets consumes energy. Loss rate can be increased by increasing the data length. Because of scheduling, larger packets might wait in the queue for a long time and the sender assumes that the packet is discarded and send the packet again.

In the same manner, throughput is dependent on loss rate, data length, delay, jitter and energy consumption. Throughput increases as the loss rate decreases. Decreasing loss rates mean that fewer packets need to be retransmitted, which in turn increases throughput. Assuming that there is no loss of data, throughput increases with the data length because fewer packets can contain more data. Throughput is increased with decreasing delay and jitter. Throughput can be decreased by low energy consumption devices.

To conclude, the criteria for selecting communication services are dependent on each other.

4.2.2.2 Choosing AHP from MCDA Methods

In the year 2000, Andrea de Montis et. al. completed an extensive survey of different MCDA methods and compared them based on the operational components of the methods, their applicability in user context and their

applicability for the problem structure. One of the operational components
of the methods was the inter-dependencies among criteria. They showed that
no other methods except AHP allows the interdependence among criteria
[79].

It is seen in Section 4.2.2.1 that inter-dependencies exist among the criteria for selecting communication services in future network architectures.
Among the presented MCDA methods, only AHP can be used for service
selection as it is the only method which supports inter-dependencies among
the selection criteria.

4.2.2.3 The Analytic Hierarchy Process (AHP)

AHP is a process designed for assisting human decision making which is
used in many application areas such as social, personal, education, manu-
facturing, political, engineering, industry and government [101]. Basically,
AHP is used for determining priorities of different alternatives.

The first step of the process is to define a hierarchy. The first and last
levels in the hierarchy contain the goal and the alternatives to choose from,
respectively. One or more levels in the middle contain evaluation criteria.

The second step is to assign pairwise priority to the criteria. The pairwise
priority is the preference or satisfaction feelings of one evaluation criterion
over another. For defining pairwise priority, a scale between 1 (equally important) to 9 (absolutely more important) is used. To make the priority
assignment easier, 5 levels in the scale are used instead of 9 levels: 1 (equally
important), 3 (moderately more important), 5 (strongly more important), 7
(very strongly more important), and 9 (extremely more important). In this

step, an $i \times j$ dimensional comparison matrix A is constructed as shown in the following equation

$$A = \begin{bmatrix} a_{11} \ a_{12} \ a_{13} \ \dots \ a_{1j} \\ a_{21} \ a_{22} \ a_{23} \ \dots \ a_{2j} \\ \cdot \\ \cdot \\ \cdot \\ a_{i1} \ a_{i2} \ a_{i3} \ \dots \ a_{ij} \end{bmatrix} \tag{4.5}$$

where $a_{ij} > 0$, $a_{ij} = 1$ when $i = j$, and $a_{ji} = \dfrac{1}{a_{ji}}$.

The next step is to calculate the overall priority value, or priority vector, which provides the relative weight among the things, or criteria, we compare. This is done in three steps. In the first step, column normalization is done according to the following equation

$$a1_{ij} = \frac{a_{ij}}{\sum_{i=1}^{n} a_{ij}} \tag{4.6}$$

In the second step, a vector is constructed by summing up the elements in each row

$$v_i = \sum_{j=1}^{n} a1_{ij} \tag{4.7}$$

In the final step, the priority vector w of each criteria i is obtained as follows

$$w_i = \frac{v_i}{j} \tag{4.8}$$

The subsequent step is to check the consistency of the priority vector by using the method proposed by Saaty, which is done in three steps. First, the largest eigenvalue of the priority matrix A, max, is calculated. Second, the consistency index $CI(n)$ is computed by using the formula

$$CI(n) = \frac{(max - n)}{(n-1)} \qquad (4.9)$$

where n is the number of criteria. Finally, the consistency ratio, $CR(n)$, is the ratio of the consistency index $CI(n)$ and the Random Consistency Index $RCI(n)$

$$CR(n) = \frac{CI(n)}{RCI(n)} \qquad (4,10)$$

The RCI for different values of n are shown in Table 4.1.

n	1	2	3	4	5	6	7	8	9
RCI	0	0	0.58	0.90	1.12	1.24	1.32	1.41	1.45

Table 4.1 Random Consistency Index

If $CR(n)$ is less than 10%, then the assignment of the pairwise priority is said to be consistent.

If the vector is not consistent, the next step is to change the pairwise priority of the criteria and repeat the process from the second step. When the vector is proved to be consistent, the priority vector of the next levels in the hierarchy is calculated.

Except for the first criteria level (i.e., the start level having criteria) in the hierarchy, the priority vector of subsequent hierarchy levels is calculated by multiplying the priority vector calculated from the nearest upper hierarchy which is consistent, and the priority vector of the hierarchy.

4.2.2.4 Adaptation of Analytic Hierarchy Process (AHP) for Service Selection

The Analytic Hierarchy Process (AHP) needs to be adapted for selecting the best communication service automatically.

To use AHP in communication service selection, the following steps need to be performed

1. Define the goal and the selection criteria for achieving the goal.
2. Pairwise priority assignment of the selection criteria as an application requirement.
3. Pairwise priority assignment of the criteria for the offered services.

The first step is to define the goal, which is to select the best communication service, and the selection criteria to achieve that goal. The selection criteria are actually a set of required effects. Examples of the selection criteria are delay, throughput, success rate, and jitter. Usually for selecting the best service, non-functional criteria are considered.

After determining the selection criteria, the next step is to assign pairwise priority between the selection criteria. One of the reasons of pairwise priority assignment is that it is easier for a person to take two criteria and to assign priority one over the other. It is initially difficult for a new application developer to assign pairwise priority. But, the efficiency of the pairwise priority assignment process can be improved with the experience of the application developer.

For n number of criteria, an application developer needs to assign $n * ((n-1)/2)$ pairwise priorities. For a small number of criteria, pairwise priority assignment might be feasible. Difficulties of pairwise priority assignment increase with increasing the number of criteria. This becomes unpractical if all of the priorities are assigned for each newly developed application.

To solve this problem, pre-defined profile (pre-assigned) for different type of applications (for example, video streaming, video on demand, and teleconferencing) can be created. The assumption here is that the selection criteria for each type of application is pre-defined and standardized. The advantage with this approach is that, an application developer does not need to assign the priorities for each newly developed application instead he may change the assignment, if required.

The third step of the process is to assign pairwise priorities between the offered services based on those selection criteria. However, as priority assignment is a time-consuming task, and as offerings are decoupled from the application, it is necessary to assign pairwise priorities automatically on the offering side.

This requires a mapping mechanism to change the measured/calculated values of the offered services to the pairwise pairwise priority assignment which will be discussed in the next section.

The calculated priority matrix coming from the application side is multiplied by the calculated priority matrix from the offering side. The result is then called the overall priority matrix. The service with the highest priority value in the overall priority matrix is the best service.

4.2.2.5 Automated priority assignment for the offerings

Different communication services can have different effects. The value (or attribute) of these effects should be obtained from the benchmarks of building blocks and sent to the broker. After gathering the measured/estimated values, for each effect, the services need to be automatically prioritized since the offerings are decoupled/hidden/out-of-reach from the application.

Therefore, an automatic mapping mechanism from measured/estimated values to the priority scale (from 1 to 9) is required.

To do that, the broker may have knowledge base containing range of values for each non-functional effect for services from different providers, the priority order including increasing (priorities increase as the value increases), or decreasing (priorities decrease as the value increases), as well as the type of distribution of those values (linear, non-linear, etc.). This knowledge base can be obtained from a standard organization including ITU, IETF (if available) or is derived from historical data. One example of such a knowledge base is shown in Table 4.2 where pseudo range of values, their distribution, and priority order is shown.

Non-functional effects	Range of values		Distribution of values	Priority order
	Minimum	Maximum		
Compression.Speed	0.01 μs	0.15 μs	linear	increasing
Compression.Ratio	0%	80%	linear	increasing
Compression.Loss	0%	5%	linear	decreasing
Decompression.Speed	0.01 μs	0.15 μs	linear	increasing
Security.KeyStrength	128 bit	256 bit	linear	increasing
Bandwidth	10 Mbps	100 Mbps	linear	increasing
Goodput	8 Mbps	98 Mbps	linear	increasing
SuccessRate	95%	100%	linear	increasing
PktErrorProbability	0%	3%	linear	decreasing
PktLossRatio	0%	0.001%	linear	decreasing
PktLossProbability	0%	10%	linear	decreasing
QueingDelay	0.05 ps	10 μs	linear	decreasing
PropagationDelay	0.001 ns	0.05 ns	linear	decreasing
TransmissionDelay	0.001 ns	0.1 ns	linear	decreasing
ProcessingDelay	0.001 ns	0.01 ns	linear	decreasing
MemoryUsage	1 MB	10 MB	linear	decreasing
CPUUsage	1 Hz	100 Hz	linear	decreasing
EnergySaving.Consumption	1 Femtowatt	100 Picowatt	linear	decreasing
ConnectionMgmt.SetUpDelay	0.001 ms	3 ms	linear	decreasing
Jitter	0.001 ms	50 ms	linear	decreasing
Throughput	8 Mbps	98 Mbps	linear	increasing
DataLoss	0%	5%	linear	decreasing

Table 4.2 Knowledge base provided in the broker

The mapping should have certain properties. First, the mapping must be generic, i.e., not specific to effects or units of measured values. Second, the mapping must be monotonic, i.e., priority values for an effect of different alternatives are either increasing or decreasing.

Two approaches for mapping are proposed here which use a monotonic interpolation/extrapolation scheme: round monotonic interpolation and fractional monotonic interpolation. Round monotonic interpolation is proposed since in AHP, pairwise priorities are assigned using absolute scale (1 to 9). The disadvantage with this approach is that, false positive best-service may be the outcome when the interval of values of effects from different services is close. To tackle that, fractional monotonic interpolation mechanism is proposed. As the difference in efficiency between these mapping mechanisms is negligible, the performance analysis of fractional monotonic interpolation mechanism is shown in Section 4.2.2.8.

In both cases, service broker has the knowledge of the value points for interpolation/extrapolation for every effect as shown in Table 4.2. Moreover, it has knowledge about the type of distribution of those values (linear, non-linear, etc). Furthermore, the broker knows based on its knowledge base whether the priority for an effect should be assigned in increasing (priorities increase as the value increases), or decreasing (priorities decrease as the value increases) order. The broker then maps from the measured/estimated values to priorities. A monotonic interpolation/extrapolation of the given points (range of values as shown in Table 4.2) by the broker is used to define a mapping. In addition, the specific measured values of the offerings are then mapped to these priorities. Assuming that $f()$ is a function used to define a mapping. As an example, considering interpolation, the broker must provide at least the following two points

- $x_0, where f(x_0) = 1$
- $x_n, where f(x_n) = 9$

If there are measurement values, y, not within the interval $[x_0, x_n]$, we can extrapolate

- $if y < x_0, then f(y) = 1$
- $if y > x_n, then f(y) = 9$

The aforementioned mapping mechanisms are used to assign a priority of one protocol graph over another for every selection criteria (effect). When adapted AHP is used to select the best building block which is necessary in composition approaches including template-based composition approach, this mechanism can also be used to assign pairwise priority of one building block over another for every selection criteria.

Round monotonic interpolation

In this case, for every effect, the broker provide hints (range of values, increasing/decreasing, distribution) for the mapping of measured values to the priority scale. These hints are shown in Table 4.2. When increasing/decreasing = decreasing (priorities decrease as the value increases) and distribution = linear, the mapping mechanism takes the measured or estimated values of a particular effect of different (building blocks or) protocol graphs and assigns priority linearly in decreasing order. The mechanism for the round monotonic interpolation is shown in Equation 4.11 when the priorities are decreased as their values increase and can be expressed by the variable priority. Only round priorities are assigned in this case. For example, 9, 8, 7, 6, 5, 4, 3, 2 and 1.

$priority = round(y) + 1$

where $y = ((value - min)/x)$, $x = ((max - min)/(n - 1))$, $min >= 0$,

$$n = 9$$
$$(4.11)$$

The variable $value$ is the measured/estimated value of a service, max and min denote the maximum and the minimum value of a criteria which is assigned by the service broker (example values shown in Table 4.2) and n denotes the maximum value of the priority scale which is 9 in this case.

$priority = round(y) + 1$

where $y = ((max - value)/x)$, $x = ((max - min)/(n - 1))$, $min >= 0$,

$$n = 9$$
$$(4.12)$$

The mechanism for the round monotonic interpolation is shown in Equation 4.12 considering increasing/decreasing = increasing (priorities increase as the value increases), and distribution = linear.

Fractional monotonic interpolation

As the name indicates, in the fractional monotonic interpolation, fractional priorities are assigned. In this case, the values of the priorities are usually floating point number, for example, 8.3, 5.2, and 1.5. Similar to the previous mechanism, it takes the measured or estimated values of a particular effect of different (building blocks or) protocol graphs, hints (range of values, increasing/decreasing, distribution) and assigns priorities accordingly.

$priority = y + 1$

where $y = ((value - min)/x)$, $x = ((max - min)/(n - 1))$, $min >= 0$,

$$n = 9$$
$$(4.13)$$

The mechanism for the fractional monotonic interpolation is shown in Equation 4.13 when increasing/decreasing = decreasing (priorities decrease as the value increases), and distribution = linear.

$$priority = y + 1$$
$$\text{where } y = ((max - value)/x), \quad x = ((max - min)/(n-1)), \quad min >= 0,$$
$$n = 9$$
$$(4.14)$$

The mechanism for the fractional monotonic interpolation is shown in Equation 4.14 when increasing/decreasing = increasing (priorities increase as the value increases), and distribution = linear.

After getting initial (pairwise) prioritization of services by using mapping mechanisms, services are pairwise prioritized for every criteria. Pairwise prioritization between services for every criteria is done by dividing the value of one service by the value of another service.

4.2.2.6 Network Abstraction API

An application programming interface (API) is required to send the application requirements to the broker and to return a suitable or the best service to the application. Affiliated with the SIG FUNCOMP, a special interest group for functional composition (selection and composition) of the German-Lab project, I created an interface titled *GAPI: A G-Lab Application-to-Network Interface* which can be used for this purpose [72].

4.2.2.7 Best Service Selection: An Example

The goal is to select the best service among three services: S1, S2 and S3. For achieving this goal, three non-functional selection criteria are chosen here: EndToEndDelay, Throughput, and, Jitter. The criteria are pairwise-prioritized as shown in Table 4.3. As it is seen in the table, EndToEndDelay is given priority as strongly more important than (5) Throughput and absolutely more important (9) than Jitter. To make the matrix consistent, Throughput and Jitter are assigned priority as strongly less important than (0.2) EndToEndDelay and absolutely less important than EndToEndDelay (0.11) respectively.

Effects	EndToEndDelay	Throughput	Jitter	Priority
EndToEndDelay	1	5	9	0.7651
Throughput	0.2	1	1	0.1288
Jitter	0.11	1	1	0.1062

Table 4.3 The requirements matrix (CR = 6.23%)

Assuming that the services S1, S2, and S3 offer the values of EndToEnd-Delay, Throughput and Jitter according to Table 4.4. The broker assigns range of values for EndToEndDelay, Throughput and Jitter are (10ms - 250ms), (1Mbps - 10Mbps), and Jitter (1ms - 10ms) respectively. In addition, it tells that the distribution of the data from different services is linear. Moreover, the broker gives hints that the priorities for EndToEndDelay and Jitter should be in decreasing order and the priority for Throughput should be in increasing order. Considering the above hints from the broker, pairwise priorities are assigned using the round monotonic interpolation method shown in Equations 4.11 and 4.12.

Services	EndToEndDelay (ms)	Throughput (Mbps)	Jitter (ms)
S1	10	1	1
S2	50	2	2
S3	250	10	10

Table 4.4 Estimated values of Services

Automatic pairwise priorities for EndToEndDelay, Throughput, and Jitter are shown in Table 4.5, 4.6, and 4.7 respectively. The overall priority is shown in Table 4.8.

Services	S1	S2	S3	Priority
S1	1	2	9	0.621
S2	0.5	1	4.5	0.310
S3	0.11	0.22	1.0	0.069

Table 4.5 Pairwise priorities for EndToEndDelay

Services	S1	S2	S3	Priority
S1	1	0.11	0.125	0.056
S2	9	1	0.125	0.237
S3	8	8	1	0.707

Table 4.6 Pairwise priorities for Throughput

Services	S1	S2	S3	Priority
S1	1	2	9	0.621
S2	0.5	1	4.5	0.310
S3	0.11	0.22	1.0	0.069

Table 4.7 Pairwise priorities for Jitter

The overall priority is obtained by multiplying the requirement matrix with the offered matrix. The service with the highest value in the overall

Requirement priorities	0.7651	0.1288	0.1062	Overall priority
	EndToEndDelay	Throughput	Jitter	
S1	0.621	0.056	0.621	0.548
S2	0.310	0.237	0.310	0.301
S3	0.069	0.707	0.069	0.151

Table 4.8 Overall priority matrix computation

priority matrix is chosen as the best service, which is S1, as shown in Table 4.8.

4.2.2.8 Efficiency of Service Selection

The mapping time and the selection time of the fractional monotonic interpolation have been measured according to the following setup.

Parameter	Value
Processor	Intel(R) Core(TM) i5-2400 CPU @ 3.10GHz 3.10GHz
OS	Windows 7 Enterprise 64-bit
Memory	4 GB
Number of selection criteria	2 to 22 (variable) shown in Table 4.2
Values of pairwise priorities between criteria	random
Number of services	2 to 100 (variable)
Values of services for each criteria	random (taken from ranges of values shown in Table 4.2)
Mapping mechanisms	fractional
Priority order	increasing, decreasing
Value recorded	Average of 1000 run

Table 4.9 Measurement and running configuration

Configuration setup

The setup of both the machine where the measurement is accomplished and the experiment itself is shown in Table 4.9. The number of selection criteria is changed from 2 to 22. Priorities between those selection criteria are assigned randomly taking values from 1 to 9.

The number of services have been increased from 2 to 100 incrementing by 1. The values for services for each effect have been taken randomly from the ranges specified in Table 4.2. For each number of service, both the mapping mechanism and the selection mechanism have been run 1000 times. The average mapping time and the selection time of those 1000 runs is then recorded in a file. Only the fractional monotonic interpolation mapping method is used to record the values. Even though the values have been recorded for 2 to 100 services, only the values of 2, 10, 20, 30, 40, 50, 60, 70, 80, 90 and 100 number services have been shown in the Figures 4.2 and 4.3.

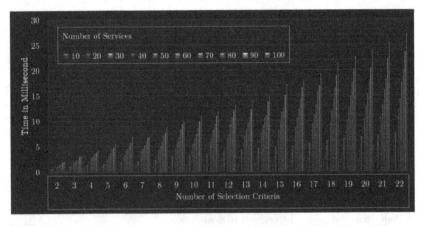

Fig. 4.2 Mapping time

Results (Mapping Time and Selection Time)

As it is seen in the Figures 4.2 and 4.3, both the mapping time and the selection time are increased linearly with the number of criteria and

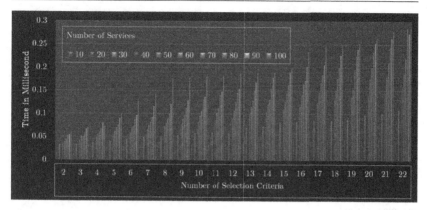

Fig. 4.3 Selection time

services provided by (building blocks or) protocol graphs. The mapping time is higher than the selection time. Mapping can be done during the runtime or beforehand, when the measured values are already available. In that case, only the selection time is considered which is scalable as it is seen in the Figure 4.3.

Considering 22 criteria, both the mapping time and selection time using the fractional monotonic interpolation method is shown in Table 4.10. As it is seen in the table, the maximum mapping time is 27 ms considering 22 criteria and 100 services. The maximum selection time is 0.285 ms considering 22 criteria and 100 services.

Currently, the mapping time and selection time is calculated by considering 22 effects and one hundred services, as today the number of networking services and selection criteria are limited. However, as both the description language and the selection mechanism are scalable, evaluation can be done in future by increasing the number of services and criteria.

As it is seen in Table 4.2, the broker assumes only linear distribution of values for an effect between different service providers. However, the broker

Number of Services	Mapping time (fractional) in ms	Selection time (fractional) in ms
10	2.709	0.049
20	4.905	0.073
30	7.492	0.109
40	10.747	0.131
50	12.15	0.157
60	14.235	0.187
70	17.331	0.22
80	20.183	0.265
90	23.505	0.274
100	27.039	0.285

Table 4.10 Mapping time and selection time using fractional monotonic interpolation mapping method

may find non-linear distribution of data in that case non-linear mapping mechanism will be required, which can be done in future.

4.2.2.9 Benefits of AHP as a Selection Method

The selection approach which uses AHP has several advantages; first, pair-wise prioritization of requirements as an input, second, consistency checking, third, benefits of relative prioritization over linear prioritization.

It is easy for people to compare two objects by using their properties. For example, a recruitment manager needs to select the best candidate for the job. One candidate has an excellent education but no working experience and the other one has a good education but has several years of experience. The manager will take these two selection criteria of the candidates (education, working experience) and can easily identify which is more important to him. If working experience is more important to him, then he will select the second candidate, otherwise, he will select the first one.

People may make mistake in assigning pairwise priority. The probability of making mistake is higher when the number of selection criteria to be prioritized increases. To overcome this problem, the analytic hierarchy process provides a way to check consistency of pairwise priority assignment. When the consistency is proved to be inconsistent, pairwise priorities are reassigned to make them consistent.

AHP uses relative prioritization rather than linear prioritization. In linear prioritization, the priority value of the requirement is assigned linearly such as (delay > throughput > loss) which means that the service with the lowest delay should be selected at first. If two services have the same delay, then the service with the highest throughput is selected. In relative prioritization, the selection criteria is pairwise prioritized. That means, a service is selected based on all of the considered criteria not only a single criterion such as in a linear prioritization technique.

5 Conclusion

Driven by future Internet projects such as GENI and FIND, the worldwide research of future network architectures results in several architectural approaches such as NENA, XIA, SONATE, RINA, and ANA, to name a few. Even though the same service with different qualities of attributes can be offered by the same architecture, the probability of having such a case can be even higher when there are many architectural approaches.

The SONATE architecture is based on the "service-orientation" principle of SOA and the "Separation of Concern" principle of Dijkstra. The idea is to break a problem into a set of sub-problems and then to solve those sub-problems separately. The solution of each of the sub-problem is then integrated to get the solution of the problem.

Similarly in SONATE, the functionalities of the TCP/IP model and the OSI model are decomposed into a set of fine-grained functionalities and to compose them based on the requirements from the application. The result is a customized network stack for every application.

For accomplishing this task, a language is required which can describe those fine-grained functionalities. The language must be generic enough so that future services can also be described. Moreover, the service should not be specific to any selection and/or composition mechanism. A communication service description language has been developed in this thesis which fulfills those constraints.

The language has been constructed by considering services offered by building blocks (the implementation of protocols or mechanisms) and constraints imposed by the networks, and requirements of an user or an application. The language consists of a taxonomy of effects and a set of rules for those effects. All of the requirements, constraints and offerings are nothing but a set of effects. For example, reliable transmission, loss detection, error detection, error correction, routing and addressing. Using the proposed language, it is possible to identify effects uniquely, and describe dependencies between/among effects. Moreover, the types of requirements (such as mandatory and optional) can be described as well. The operators usage in the language provides the capability to compare the effects. Using aggregations, it is possible to identify the amount of a particular property (for example, Minimum MTU, Maximum Delay, Aggregated Throughput). Units offer the ability to express the amount in a particular unit (for example, Delay in ms, Cost in Euro).

The language has been implemented using Resource Description Framework (RDF) which is a standard language recommended by world wide web community and XML Schema. RDF has some powerful features such as URI which assigns each item of the language such as effects, interfaces, datatypes, operators and units uniquely and sequence is used for arranging services in a particular order. URI solves incompatibility issues when services to compose come from different developers and providers by identifying each service uniquely. Using RDF, logical operators and inference can not be expressed. For having those features in the language, it is possible to integrate web ontology language (OWL) on the top of RDF. This concludes that, the language is easily extensible based on the demands in the future.

All of the selection and composition mechanisms to create protocol graphs can get benefit from the language proposed in this thesis.

Using different composition mechanisms in SONATE, services which fulfill the application (suitable services) requirements can be returned to the broker. In this thesis, suitable services are selected just by matching the description of the offered services with the application requirements. This thesis also contributes to the selection of the best service.

Selecting the best service using a single criterion is trivial. For example, considering a single selection criterion delay, the best service is the one which has the lowest delay. However, communication services have multiple selection criteria. Therefore, selecting the best service is a multi-criteria decision making problem.

For solving such a problem, different multi-criteria decision analysis methods exist in management science. For example, MAUT, AHP, Evamix, Regime, ELECTRE III, NAIADE and MOP/GP. The Analytic Hierarchy Process (AHP) is chosen for the communication service selection as it supports relative prioritization and checks consistency.

However, the process is required to be adapted for communication service selection. In a service oriented network architecture, offerings are decoupled from the application. Therefore, the measured or estimated values of the offered services need to be mapped based on hints assigned by the broker. This is done by the proposed mapping mechanisms named "round monotonic interpolation" and "fractional monotonic interpolation".

The process of selecting the best service is implemented in the Java programming language and evaluated using twenty two selection criteria (effects) and one hundred offered services.

When the mapping is done beforehand, the result shows that 0.285 milliseconds are required to select the best service between one hundred offered services using twenty two selection criteria.

All of the selection and composition mechanisms to create protocol graphs can get benefit from the selection mechanisms proposed in this thesis.

To conclude, applications use networks differently, and therefore have different network requirements. At the same time, networking capabilities and protocols make advances. This thesis shows how applications can make use of advancing network capabilities by specifying requirements and using a selection process to choose the best available communication service.

Describing application requirements and communication services supports the parallel development of both applications and communication services, which leads to the evolution of the Internet. As soon as new protocols or networks emerge that fulfill the application requirements, they can be automatically selected by using the service selection process.

Both the description language and the selection mechanisms can be used in any place where communication service description and selection is required.

6 Benefits and Future Work

The proposed description language has several advantages; 1, it provides a generic syntax so that all of the current application requirements, network offerings, and administrator constraints can be expressed, 2, the language is extensible with new vocabularies and new syntax, 3, the language can be used in any place where communication service description is required.

The selection approach which uses AHP has several advantages; first, pairwise prioritization of requirements as an input, second, consistency checking, third, benefits of relative prioritization over linear prioritization.

Decoupling applications and network stacks is achieved by using the proposed description language and service selection methods. Using the language, the requirements from the applications and the capabilities of the network stacks can be described. Using the service selection method, both suitable network stacks based on application requirements and when several suitable network stacks available, the best network stack can be selected. Therefore, using the language and selection methods, applications and networks can be evolved in a decoupled manner.

In this thesis, two mapping mechanisms have been proposed (namely, round monotonic interpolation and fractional monotonic interpolation) for assigning pairwise priorities automatically between offered services for every selection criteria. These mechanisms assign priorities linearly which might not be appropriate for services when non-linear priorities are necessary to be assigned. In future, effects and services may be categorized based on their linear and non-linear relationships and provide mapping mechanisms for effects (and services) that require non-linear mappings.

A Appendix

A.1 Examples of Communication Services

Some examples of communication services are given below:

- **Security:** Security is one of the most popular and necessary communication services which mean that the data is kept safe from intruders/middle-man during communication. This service is necessary for online banking transactions, military communication, medical communication, emergency needs and much more. There are several security services: *integrity, data-origin authentication and confidentiality. Data origin authentication* is a security service that verifies the identity of the claimed source of data. This ensures that the information is sent to or from a trusted partner. *Integrity* is a security service that ensures that modifications to the data are detectable. Even if the intruder obtains the information, *confidentiality* ensures that the man-in-the-middle cannot understand the information by changing the information into an unintelligible form. Users can ask either request *Security* in general or one or more of those security services: data-origin authentication, integrity, or confidentiality. Here, it is assumed that, when users request the *Security* service, all of those security services will be provided.

- **Routing:** This service, in general, routes the packet from source to destination.

- **RTT_Information:** User or application can get Round Trip Time information by using this service.

- **Hop_Information:** Using this service, users or applications can get the number of hops between the sender and the receiver.

- **Addressing_Conversion:** Using this service, the addresses can be converted from one type to another. For example, from IPv4 to IPv6 address.

- **Prioritization:** When the user or the application needs to give priority of one class of traffic to another, this service can be used.

- **Signal_Conversion:** In case the application needs to convert from one signal type to another, this service can be used, for instance, conversion from analog to digital signal or the other way around.

- **Size_Reduction:** If the application cannot send a file because of its size, a Size Reduction service can be taken to do the task. Compression is one type of size reduction service. The user can request for either of the services to get the desired task done.

- **Availability:** Availability covers different services. The most common one is monitoring which observes whether the peer host is still up and the connection is still alive. Employing the monitoring service as a foundation, a path management service can be created. These can have two different types: the basic one is multihoming. In this case, there are multiple available paths. If for certain circumstances, one path fails, it switches to another path that is not erroneous. A drawback of this service is that always only one path is active. There is a service called *Load_Sharing* which uses different paths simultaneously. Another availability service is

Denial-of-Service availability *(DoS_Availability)* which ensures that the authorized users are still able to get served even when the system is under attack. Users can ask explicitly for one or more of the availability services or for the *Availability* service in general when only the Monitoring service will be provided.

- **Addressing:** This is a common communication service that identifies the source and destination process and its devices. Users or applications can request for one or more of the addressing services explicitly.

- **Connection_Management:** This service provides connection management including connection establishment and connection termination. Users or applications can explicitly request either of the services or in general *Connection_Management* where both of the services will be provided.

- **Reliability:** The Reliability service ensures that the data must reach the destination without any corruption. There are several reliability services: *error detection, data flow limiting, order preservation* and *error control*. As the name indicates, error detection service detects errors that have been happened on the way. Data flow limiting is an important service in a shared network which is used to avoid source, destination and network congestion by limiting data flow. The order preservation service ensures that the data arrives at the destination in the same order as the data has been sent. When *Reliability* service in general is requested, all of the reliability services will be provided. But, the user can clearly ask for one or more of the reliability services for decreasing the cost of communication.

- **Packet_Boundaries_Preservation:** In case of user or application needs, this service ensures that the packet will not be segmented or fragmented.

- **Path_MTU:** This service provides the size of the maximum transfer unit between the source and the destination.

- **Loop_Avoidance:** This service avoids loop during routing data.

A.2 Components of Communication Service Description Language (CSDL)

The following code describes the *DataType* component of the language

```
<?xml version="1.0" encoding="UTF-8"?>
<rdf:RDF xmlns:rdf="http://www.w3.org/1999/02/22-rdf-syntax-ns
    #"
xmlns:sonate="http://www.icsy.de/sonate-ns#">
  <rdf:Description rdf:about="sonate/Effects/DataType">
    <sonate:name>DataType</sonate:name>
    <sonate:info>Describes the types of data, which is
        necessary
                for validating interfaces</sonate:info>
    <sonate:category>
      <rdf:Bag>
        <rdf:li>
          <rdf:Description rdf:about="sonate/Effects/DataType/
              Integer">
            <sonate:name>Integer</sonate:name>
            <sonate:info>The type of data is integer</sonate:
                info>
          </rdf:Description>
        </rdf:li>
        <rdf:li>
          <rdf:Description rdf:about="sonate/Effects/DataType/
              Real">
            <sonate:name>Real</sonate:name>
```

```
      <sonate:info>The type of data is real</sonate:info>
    </rdf:Description>
  </rdf:li>
  <rdf:li>
    <rdf:Description rdf:about="sonate/Effects/DataType/
      String">
      <sonate:name>String</sonate:name>
      <sonate:info>The type of data is string</sonate:
        info>
    </rdf:Description>
  </rdf:li>
  <rdf:li>
    <rdf:Description rdf:about="sonate/Effects/DataType/
      Char">
      <sonate:name>Char</sonate:name>
      <sonate:info>The type of data is char</sonate:info>
    </rdf:Description>
  </rdf:li>
  <rdf:li>
    <rdf:Description rdf:about="sonate/Effects/DataType/
      ByteArray">
      <sonate:name>ByteArray</sonate:name>
      <sonate:info>The type of data is a ByteArray</
        sonate:info>
    </rdf:Description>
  </rdf:li>
  <rdf:li>
    <rdf:Description rdf:about="sonate/Effects/DataType/
      Array">
      <sonate:name>Array</sonate:name>
      <sonate:info>The type of data is an array</sonate:
        info>
    </rdf:Description>
  </rdf:li>
```

```
    </rdf:Bag>
  </sonate:category>
 </rdf:Description>
</rdf:RDF>
```

The following code describes the *Dependencies* component of the language

```
<?xml version="1.0" encoding="UTF-8"?>
<rdf:RDF xmlns:rdf="http://www.w3.org/1999/02/22-rdf-syntax-ns
    #" xmlns:sonate="http://www.icsy.de/sonate-ns#">
  <rdf:Description rdf:about="sonate/Effects/Dependencies">
    <sonate:name>Dependencies</sonate:name>
    <sonate:info>Describes dependency types, dependency order,
        depedency
                   targets (dependency between BBs or Services
                   ) and
                   dependeny purpose (Requirement or Ordering)
                   </sonate:info>
    <sonate:category>
      <rdf:Bag>
        <rdf:li>
          <rdf:Description rdf:about="sonate/Effects/
            Dependencies/Types">
            <sonate:name>Types</sonate:name>
            <sonate:info>Dependency types (Hard/Soft)</sonate:
              info>
            <sonate:category>
              <rdf:Bag>
                <rdf:li>
                  <rdf:Description rdf:about="sonate/Effects/
                    Dependencies/Types/Soft">
                    <sonate:name>Soft</sonate:name>
                    <sonate:info>Fulfilling this dependency is
                      optional</sonate:info>
```

```
        </rdf:Description>
      </rdf:li>
      <rdf:li>
        <rdf:Description rdf:about="sonate/Effects/
          Dependencies/Types/Hard">
          <sonate:name>Hard</sonate:name>
          <sonate:info>Fulfilling this dependency is a
            must</sonate:info>
        </rdf:Description>
      </rdf:li>
    </rdf:Bag>
  </sonate:category>
</rdf:Description>
</rdf:li>
<rdf:li>
  <rdf:Description rdf:about="sonate/Effects/
    Dependencies/Order">
    <sonate:name>Order</sonate:name>
    <sonate:info>Dependency order (Sequence/
      MutualExclusion/Unordered)</sonate:info>
    <sonate:category>
      <rdf:Bag>
        <rdf:li>
          <rdf:Description rdf:about="sonate/Effects/
            Dependencies/Order/Sequence">
            <sonate:name>Sequence</sonate:name>
            <sonate:info>Specific sequence of
              functionality</sonate:info>
          </rdf:Description>
        </rdf:li>
        <rdf:li>
          <rdf:Description rdf:about="sonate/Effects/
            Dependencies/Order/MutualExclusion">
            <sonate:name>MutualExclusion</sonate:name>
```

```
                    <sonate:info>Functionalities are mutually
                        exclusive</sonate:info>
                    </rdf:Description>
                </rdf:li>
                <rdf:li>
                  <rdf:Description rdf:about="sonate/Effects/
                      Dependencies/Order/Unordered">
                    <sonate:name>Unordered</sonate:name>
                    <sonate:info>Functionalities are unordered</
                        sonate:info>
                    </rdf:Description>
                </rdf:li>
              </rdf:Bag>
            </sonate:category>
          </rdf:Description>
        </rdf:li>
        <rdf:li>
          <rdf:Description rdf:about="sonate/Effects/
              Dependencies/Target">
            <sonate:name>Target</sonate:name>
            <sonate:info>Dependency target (BB-BB/BB-S/S-S)</
                sonate:info>
            <sonate:category>
              <rdf:Bag>
                <rdf:li>
                  <rdf:Description rdf:about="sonate/Effects/
                      Dependencies/Target/BB">
                    <sonate:name>BB</sonate:name>
                    <sonate:info>Dependency exists between a BB
                        and a BB or a Service</sonate:info>
                    </rdf:Description>
                </rdf:li>
                <rdf:li>
```

```
            <rdf:Description rdf:about="sonate/Effects/
                Dependencies/Target/Service">
              <sonate:name>Service</sonate:name>
              <sonate:info>Dependency exists between a
                  Service and a BB or a Service</sonate:
                  info>
            </rdf:Description>
          </rdf:li>
        </rdf:Bag>
      </sonate:category>
    </rdf:Description>
  </rdf:li>
  <rdf:li>
    <rdf:Description rdf:about="sonate/Effects/
        Dependencies/Purpose">
      <sonate:name>Purpose</sonate:name>
      <sonate:info>Purpose of dependencies (Requirements
          or ordering or both)</sonate:info>
      <sonate:category>
        <rdf:Bag>
          <rdf:li>
            <rdf:Description rdf:about="sonate/Effects/
                Dependencies/Purpose/Requirement">
              <sonate:name>Requirement</sonate:name>
              <sonate:info>Requirement dependency</sonate:
                  info>
            </rdf:Description>
          </rdf:li>
          <rdf:li>
            <rdf:Description rdf:about="sonate/Effects/
                Dependencies/Purpose/Ordering">
              <sonate:name>Ordering</sonate:name>
              <sonate:info>Ordering dependency</sonate:
                  info>
```

```
            </rdf:Description>
          </rdf:li>
        </rdf:Bag>
      </sonate:category>
    </rdf:Description>
  </rdf:li>
  <rdf:li>
    <rdf:Description rdf:about="sonate/Effects/
        Dependencies/Location">
      <sonate:name>Location</sonate:name>
      <sonate:info>Location of the dependent components (
          BB or Service)</sonate:info>
      <sonate:category>
        <rdf:Bag>
          <rdf:li>
            <rdf:Description rdf:about="sonate/Effects/
                Dependencies/Location/Local">
              <sonate:name>Local</sonate:name>
              <sonate:info>The dependent component resides
                  locally</sonate:info>
            </rdf:Description>
          </rdf:li>
          <rdf:li>
            <rdf:Description rdf:about="sonate/Effects/
                Dependencies/Location/EndPoint">
              <sonate:name>EndPoint</sonate:name>
              <sonate:info>The dependent component resides
                  on the end point or receiver
                            </sonate:info>
            </rdf:Description>
          </rdf:li>
          <rdf:li>
            <rdf:Description rdf:about="sonate/Effects/
                Dependencies/Location/MiddleBox">
```

```
          <sonate:name>MiddleBox</sonate:name>
          <sonate:info>The dependent component resides
          on the network (router,
                              switch)</sonate:info>
       </rdf:Description>
      </rdf:li>
     </rdf:Bag>
    </sonate:category>
   </rdf:Description>
  </rdf:li>
 </rdf:Bag>
</sonate:category>
</rdf:Description>
</rdf:RDF>
```

The following code describes the *Effect* component of the language

```
<?xml version="1.0" encoding="UTF-8"?>
<rdf:RDF xmlns:rdf="http://www.w3.org/1999/02/22-rdf-syntax-ns
    #" xmlns:sonate="http://www.icsy.de/sonate-ns#">
  <rdf:Description rdf:about="sonate/Effects">
    <sonate:name>Effects</sonate:name>
    <sonate:info>Effects</sonate:info>
    <sonate:has>Dependencies</sonate:has>
    <sonate:has>EffectsSpecification</sonate:has>
    <sonate:has>Interface</sonate:has>
    <sonate:has>DataType</sonate:has>
    <sonate:has>Influence</sonate:has>
    <sonate:has>Operators</sonate:has>
    <sonate:has>Types</sonate:has>
    <sonate:has>Metrics</sonate:has>
    <sonate:has>Units</sonate:has>
  </rdf:Description>
</rdf:RDF>
```

The following code describes the *EffectsSpecification* component of the
language

```xml
<?xml version="1.0" encoding="UTF-8"?>
<rdf:RDF xmlns:rdf="http://www.w3.org/1999/02/22-rdf-syntax-ns
    #" xmlns:sonate="http://www.icsy.de/sonate-ns#">
  <rdf:Description rdf:about="sonate/Effects/
    EffectsSpecification">
  <sonate:name>EffectsSpecification</sonate:name>
  <sonate:info>Names/IDs/URIs of effects</sonate:info>
  <sonate:category>
    <rdf:Bag>
      <rdf:li>
        <rdf:Description rdf:about="sonate/Effects/
          EffectsSpecification/Delay">
        <sonate:name>Delay</sonate:name>
        <sonate:info>Delay of packets</sonate:info>
        <sonate:category>
          <rdf:Bag>
            <rdf:li>
              <rdf:Description rdf:about="sonate/Effects/
                EffectsSpecification/Delay/ProcessingDelay
                ">
              <sonate:name>ProcessingDelay</sonate:name>
              <sonate:info>Time for processing a packet</
                sonate:info>
              </rdf:Description>
            </rdf:li>
            <rdf:li>
              <rdf:Description rdf:about="sonate/Effects/
                EffectsSpecification/Delay/QueingDelay">
              <sonate:name>QueingDelay</sonate:name>
              <sonate:info>Time consumed for waiting in
                the queue</sonate:info>
```

```
        </rdf:Description>
      </rdf:li>
      <rdf:li>
        <rdf:Description rdf:about="sonate/Effects/
          EffectsSpecification/Delay/
          PropagationDelay">
          <sonate:name>PropagationDelay</sonate:name>
          <sonate:info>Time consumed for propagation
            of a packet from source to destination <
            /sonate:info>
        </rdf:Description>
      </rdf:li>
      </rdf:Bag>
    </sonate:category>
  </rdf:Description>
</rdf:li>
<rdf:li>
  <rdf:Description rdf:about="sonate/Effects/
    EffectsSpecification/Jitter">
    <sonate:name>Jitter</sonate:name>
    <sonate:info>Variations in delay of packets
      arriving at the destination </sonate:info>
  </rdf:Description>
</rdf:li>
<rdf:li>
  <rdf:Description rdf:about="sonate/Effects/
    EffectsSpecification/NumPacketsSent">
    <sonate:name>NumPacketsSent</sonate:name>
    <sonate:info>Number of packets sent</sonate:info>
  </rdf:Description>
</rdf:li>
<rdf:li>
  <rdf:Description rdf:about="sonate/Effects/
    EffectsSpecification/NumPacketsArrived">
```

```
      <sonate:name>NumPacketsArrived</sonate:name>
      <sonate:info>Number of packets arrived</sonate:info
         >
   </rdf:Description>
</rdf:li>
<rdf:li>
   <rdf:Description rdf:about="sonate/Effects/
      EffectsSpecification/TimePacketsSent">
      <sonate:name>TimePacketsSent</sonate:name>
      <sonate:info>Time of sending packets</sonate:info>
   </rdf:Description>
</rdf:li>
<rdf:li>
   <rdf:Description rdf:about="sonate/Effects/
      EffectsSpecification/TimePacketsArrived">
      <sonate:name>TimePacketsArrived</sonate:name>
      <sonate:info>Time of arrived packets</sonate:info>
   </rdf:Description>
</rdf:li>
<rdf:li>
   <rdf:Description rdf:about="sonate/Effects/
      EffectsSpecification/LossRatio">
      <sonate:name>LossRatio</sonate:name>
      <sonate:info>((Lost packets) / Total number of
         sending packets)*100</sonate:info>
   </rdf:Description>
</rdf:li>
<rdf:li>
   <rdf:Description rdf:about="sonate/Effects/
      EffectsSpecification/SuccessRate">
      <sonate:name>SuccessRate</sonate:name>
      <sonate:info>((Success fully arrived packets) /
         Total number of sending packets)*100</sonate:
         info>
```

```
    </rdf:Description>
  </rdf:li>
  <rdf:li>
    <rdf:Description rdf:about="sonate/Effects/
      EffectsSpecification/MTU">
      <sonate:name>MTU</sonate:name>
      <sonate:info>Maximum Transfer Unit (i.e., maximum
        size of a packet)
                 </sonate:info>
    </rdf:Description>
  </rdf:li>
  <rdf:li>
    <rdf:Description rdf:about="sonate/Effects/
      EffectsSpecification/CPU-Usage">
      <sonate:name>CPU-Usage</sonate:name>
      <sonate:info>Usage of CPU</sonate:info>
    </rdf:Description>
  </rdf:li>
  <rdf:li>
    <rdf:Description rdf:about="sonate/Effects/
      EffectsSpecification/Energy">
      <sonate:name>Energy</sonate:name>
      <sonate:info>Energy provided by a device, antenna
        and requested for a particular application</
        sonate:info>
    </rdf:Description>
  </rdf:li>
  <rdf:li>
    <rdf:Description rdf:about="sonate/Effects/
      EffectsSpecification/AccessTechnologies">
      <sonate:name>AccessTechnologies</sonate:name>
      <sonate:info>Access Technologies like WLAN, UMTS,
        HSPDA, GPRS, GSM, Broadband, EDGE</sonate:info>
    </rdf:Description>
```

```
        </rdf:li>
        <rdf:li>
          <rdf:Description rdf:about="sonate/Effects/
            EffectsSpecification/Bandwidth">
            <sonate:name>Bandwidth</sonate:name>
            <sonate:info>Bandwidth</sonate:info>
          </rdf:Description>
        </rdf:li>
        <rdf:li>
          <rdf:Description rdf:about="sonate/Effects/
            EffectsSpecification/Throughput">
            <sonate:name>Throughput</sonate:name>
            <sonate:info>Throughput</sonate:info>
          </rdf:Description>
        </rdf:li>
      </rdf:Bag>
    </sonate:category>
  </rdf:Description>
</rdf:RDF>
```

The following code describes the *Influence* component of the language

```
<?xml version="1.0" encoding="UTF-8"?>
<rdf:RDF xmlns:rdf="http://www.w3.org/1999/02/22-rdf-syntax-ns
    #" xmlns:sonate="http://www.icsy.de/sonate-ns#">
  <rdf:Description rdf:about="sonate/Effects/Influence">
    <sonate:name>Influence</sonate:name>
    <sonate:info>Describes whether an effect influences an
        header of a packet, a payload of a packet, packet as a
        whole or the flow of a packet</sonate:info>
    <sonate:category>
      <rdf:Bag>
        <rdf:li>
          <rdf:Description rdf:about="sonate/Effects/Influence/
            Flow">
            <sonate:name>Flow</sonate:name>
```

```
<sonate:info>Influences flow of packets</sonate:
   info>
<sonate:category>
 <rdf:Bag>
  <rdf:li>
    <rdf:Description rdf:about="sonate/Effects/
       Influence/Flow/Packet">
     <sonate:name>Packet</sonate:name>
     <sonate:info>Influences a packet</sonate:
        info>
     <sonate:category>
      <rdf:Bag>
       <rdf:li>
         <rdf:Description rdf:about="sonate/
            Effects/Influence/Flow/Packet/
            Header">
          <sonate:name>Header</sonate:name>
          <sonate:info>Influences an header of
             a packet</sonate:info>
         </rdf:Description>
       </rdf:li>
       <rdf:li>
         <rdf:Description rdf:about="sonate/
            Effects/Influence/Flow/Packet/
            Payload">
          <sonate:name>Payload</sonate:name>
          <sonate:info>Influences the payload
             of a packet</sonate:info>
         </rdf:Description>
       </rdf:li>
      </rdf:Bag>
     </sonate:category>
    </rdf:Description>
  </rdf:li>
```

```
        </rdf:Bag>
      </sonate:category>
      </rdf:Description>
    </rdf:li>
  </rdf:Bag>
  </sonate:category>
  </rdf:Description>
</rdf:RDF>
```

The following code describes the *Interface* component of the language

```
<?xml version="1.0" encoding="UTF-8"?>
<rdf:RDF xmlns:rdf="http://www.w3.org/1999/02/22-rdf-syntax-ns
    #" xmlns:sonate="http://www.icsy.de/sonate-ns#">
  <rdf:Description rdf:about="sonate/Effects/Interface">
    <sonate:name>Interface</sonate:name>
    <sonate:info>Describes the interfaces through which the
        effects can
                    be accessed</sonate:info>
    <sonate:category>
      <rdf:Bag>
        <rdf:li>
          <rdf:Description rdf:about="sonate/Effects/Interface/
            Up">
            <sonate:name>Up</sonate:name>
            <sonate:info>The interface is located on the top of
                the building block and receives data from the
                Down inteface of the upper building block</
                sonate:info>
          </rdf:Description>
        </rdf:li>
        <rdf:li>
          <rdf:Description rdf:about="sonate/Effects/Interface/
            Down">
            <sonate:name>Down</sonate:name>
```

```
          <sonate:info>The interface is located on the bottom
              of the building block and sends data to the Up
              interface of the building block which is in
              the beneath of this building block</sonate:info
              >
        </rdf:Description>
      </rdf:li>
      <rdf:li>
        <rdf:Description rdf:about="sonate/Effects/Interface/
            Management">
          <sonate:name>Management</sonate:name>
          <sonate:info>This interface is used for management
              purpose, for example, receiving loss rate</
              sonate:info>
        </rdf:Description>
      </rdf:li>
    </rdf:Bag>
  </sonate:category>
 </rdf:Description>
</rdf:RDF>
```

The following code describes the *Metrics* component of the language

```
<?xml version="1.0" encoding="UTF-8"?>
<rdf:RDF xmlns:rdf="http://www.w3.org/1999/02/22-rdf-syntax-ns
    #" xmlns:sonate="http://www.icsy.de/sonate-ns#">
  <rdf:Description rdf:about="sonate/Effects/Metrics">
    <sonate:name>Metrics</sonate:name>
    <sonate:info>Metrics of different properties (delay,
        throughput)</sonate:info>
    <sonate:category>
      <rdf:Bag>
        <rdf:li>
          <rdf:Description rdf:about="sonate/Effects/Metrics/
              Minimum">
            <sonate:name>Minimum</sonate:name>
```

```
      <sonate:info>Minimum value of a property</sonate:
         info>
   </rdf:Description>
</rdf:li>
<rdf:li>
   <rdf:Description rdf:about="sonate/Effects/Metrics/
      Maximum">
      <sonate:name>Maximum</sonate:name>
      <sonate:info>Maximum value of a property</sonate:
         info>
   </rdf:Description>
</rdf:li>
<rdf:li>
   <rdf:Description rdf:about="sonate/Effects/Metrics/
      Average">
      <sonate:name>Average</sonate:name>
      <sonate:info>Average value of a property</sonate:
         info>
   </rdf:Description>
</rdf:li>
<rdf:li>
   <rdf:Description rdf:about="sonate/Effects/Metrics/
      Aggregated">
      <sonate:name>Aggregated</sonate:name>
      <sonate:info>Aggregated value of a property</sonate
         :info>
   </rdf:Description>
</rdf:li>
<rdf:li>
   <rdf:Description rdf:about="sonate/Effects/Metrics/
      Interval">
      <sonate:name>Interval</sonate:name>
      <sonate:info>Values between lower bound and upper
         bound</sonate:info>
```

```
      </rdf:Description>
    </rdf:li>
    <rdf:li>
      <rdf:Description rdf:about="sonate/Effects/Metrics/
        Rating">
        <sonate:name>Rating</sonate:name>
        <sonate:info>Rated value</sonate:info>
      </rdf:Description>
    </rdf:li>
    <rdf:li>
      <rdf:Description rdf:about="sonate/Effects/Metrics/
        Scaling">
        <sonate:name>Scaling</sonate:name>
        <sonate:info>A scale in a particular range (for
          example, +9, -9) where a specific value is
          measured</sonate:info>
      </rdf:Description>
    </rdf:li>
    <rdf:li>
      <rdf:Description rdf:about="sonate/Effects/Metrics/
        Available">
        <sonate:name>Available</sonate:name>
        <sonate:info>Available bandwidth, energy,
          throughput</sonate:info>
      </rdf:Description>
    </rdf:li>
    </rdf:Bag>
  </sonate:category>
  </rdf:Description>
</rdf:RDF>
```

The following code describes the *Operators* component of the language

```
<?xml version="1.0" encoding="UTF-8"?>
<rdf:RDF xmlns:rdf="http://www.w3.org/1999/02/22-rdf-syntax-ns
  #" xmlns:sonate="http://www.icsy.de/sonate-ns#">
```

```
<rdf:Description rdf:about="sonate/Effects/Operators">
  <sonate:name>Operators</sonate:name>
  <sonate:info>Mathmetical and logical operators</sonate:
    info>
  <sonate:category>
    <rdf:Bag>
      <rdf:li>
        <rdf:Description rdf:about="sonate/Effects/Operators/
          Math">
          <sonate:name>Math</sonate:name>
          <sonate:info>Mathmetical operators</sonate:info>
          <sonate:category>
            <rdf:Bag>
              <rdf:li>
                <rdf:Description rdf:about="sonate/Effects/
                  Operators/Math/Equal">
                  <sonate:name>Equal</sonate:name>
                  <sonate:info>Equal operator (A Equal B)</
                    sonate:info>
                </rdf:Description>
              </rdf:li>
              <rdf:li>
                <rdf:Description rdf:about="sonate/Effects/
                  Operators/Math/GreaterThan">
                  <sonate:name>GreaterThan</sonate:name>
                  <sonate:info>GreaterThan operator (A
                    GreaterThan B)</sonate:info>
                </rdf:Description>
              </rdf:li>
              <rdf:li>
                <rdf:Description rdf:about="sonate/Effects/
                  Operators/Math/LessThan">
                  <sonate:name>LessThan</sonate:name>
```

```
            <sonate:info>LessThan operator (A LessThan B
                )</sonate:info>
            </rdf:Description>
          </rdf:li>
        </rdf:Bag>
      </sonate:category>
    </rdf:Description>
  </rdf:li>
  <rdf:li>
    <rdf:Description rdf:about="sonate/Effects/Operators/
      Logical">
      <sonate:name>Logical</sonate:name>
      <sonate:info>Logical operators</sonate:info>
      <sonate:category>
        <rdf:Bag>
          <rdf:li>
            <rdf:Description rdf:about="sonate/Effects/
              Operators/Logical/AND">
              <sonate:name>AND</sonate:name>
              <sonate:info>Logical AND operator (A AND B)<
                /sonate:info>
            </rdf:Description>
          </rdf:li>
          <rdf:li>
            <rdf:Description rdf:about="sonate/Effects/
              Operators/Logical/OR">
              <sonate:name>OR</sonate:name>
              <sonate:info>Logical OR operator (A OR B)</
                sonate:info>
            </rdf:Description>
          </rdf:li>
          <rdf:li>
            <rdf:Description rdf:about="sonate/Effects/
              Operators/Logical/NOT">
```

```
                    <sonate:name>NOT</sonate:name>
                    <sonate:info>Logical NOT operator (NOT A)</
                        sonate:info>
                  </rdf:Description>
                </rdf:li>
                <rdf:li>
                  <rdf:Description rdf:about="sonate/Effects/
                      Operators/Logical/XOR">
                    <sonate:name>XOR</sonate:name>
                    <sonate:info>Logical XOR operator (A XOR B)<
                        /sonate:info>
                  </rdf:Description>
                </rdf:li>
              </rdf:Bag>
            </sonate:category>
          </rdf:Description>
        </rdf:li>
      </rdf:Bag>
    </sonate:category>
  </rdf:Description>
</rdf:RDF>
```

The following code describes the *Types* component of the language

```
<?xml version="1.0" encoding="UTF-8"?>
<rdf:RDF xmlns:rdf="http://www.w3.org/1999/02/22-rdf-syntax-ns
    #" xmlns:sonate="http://www.icsy.de/sonate-ns#">
  <rdf:Description rdf:about="sonate/Effects/Types">
    <sonate:name>Types</sonate:name>
    <sonate:info>Types (Mandatory/Optional) of effects</sonate
        :info>
    <sonate:category>
      <rdf:Bag>
        <rdf:li>
          <rdf:Description rdf:about="sonate/Effects/Types/
              Mandatory">
```

```
          <sonate:name>Mandatory</sonate:name>
          <sonate:info>Mandatory properties must be fulfilled
              </sonate:info>
        </rdf:Description>
      </rdf:li>
      <rdf:li>
        <rdf:Description rdf:about="sonate/Effects/Types/
            Optional">
          <sonate:name>Optional</sonate:name>
          <sonate:info>Fulfilling optional properties are not
              required and is used for optimization</sonate:
              info>
        </rdf:Description>
      </rdf:li>
    </rdf:Bag>
  </sonate:category>
</rdf:Description>
</rdf:RDF>
```

The following code describes the *Units* component of the language

```
<?xml version="1.0" encoding="UTF-8"?>
<rdf:RDF xmlns:rdf="http://www.w3.org/1999/02/22-rdf-syntax-ns
    #" xmlns:sonate="http://www.icsy.de/sonate-ns#">
  <rdf:Description rdf:about="sonate/Properties/Units">
    <sonate:name>Units</sonate:name>
    <sonate:info>Units of properties</sonate:info>
    <sonate:category>
      <rdf:Bag>
        <rdf:li>
          <rdf:Description rdf:about="sonate/Properties/Units/
              TimeUnit">
            <sonate:name>TimeUnit</sonate:name>
            <sonate:info>Time units</sonate:info>
            <sonate:category>
              <rdf:Bag>
```

```
          <rdf:li>
            <rdf:Description rdf:about="sonate/Properties/
                Units/TimeUnit/s">
              <sonate:name>s</sonate:name>
              <sonate:info>Second</sonate:info>
            </rdf:Description>
          </rdf:li>
          <rdf:li>
            <rdf:Description rdf:about="sonate/Properties/
                Units/TimeUnit/ms">
              <sonate:name>ms</sonate:name>
              <sonate:info>millisecond</sonate:info>
            </rdf:Description>
          </rdf:li>
        </rdf:Bag>
      </sonate:category>
    </rdf:Description>
  </rdf:li>
  <rdf:li>
    <rdf:Description rdf:about="sonate/Properties/Units/
        SizeUnit">
      <sonate:name>SizeUnit</sonate:name>
      <sonate:info>Size units</sonate:info>
      <sonate:category>
        <rdf:Bag>
          <rdf:li>
            <rdf:Description rdf:about="sonate/Properties/
                Units/SizeUnit/bit">
              <sonate:name>bit</sonate:name>
              <sonate:info>binary digit</sonate:info>
            </rdf:Description>
          </rdf:li>
          <rdf:li>
```

```
                    <rdf:Description rdf:about="sonate/Properties/
                        Units/SizeUnit/">
                      <sonate:name>Byte</sonate:name>
                      <sonate:info>1 Byte = 8 bits</sonate:info>
                    </rdf:Description>
                  </rdf:li>
                  <rdf:li>
                    <rdf:Description rdf:about="sonate/Properties/
                        Units/SizeUnit/">
                      <sonate:name>KB</sonate:name>
                      <sonate:info>1 KByte = 1024*8 bits</sonate:
                        info>
                    </rdf:Description>
                  </rdf:li>
                  <rdf:li>
                    <rdf:Description rdf:about="sonate/Properties/
                        Units/SizeUnit/">
                      <sonate:name>MB</sonate:name>
                      <sonate:info>1 MByte = 1024*1024*8 bits</
                        sonate:info>
                    </rdf:Description>
                  </rdf:li>
                  <rdf:li>
                    <rdf:Description rdf:about="sonate/Properties/
                        Units/SizeUnit/">
                      <sonate:name>MB</sonate:name>
                      <sonate:info>1 GByte = 1024*1024*1024*8 bits
                        </sonate:info>
                    </rdf:Description>
                  </rdf:li>
                </rdf:Bag>
              </sonate:category>
            </rdf:Description>
          </rdf:li>
```

```
<rdf:li>
  <rdf:Description rdf:about="sonate/Properties/Units/
    SpeedUnit">
   <sonate:name>SpeedUnit</sonate:name>
   <sonate:info>Units for speed</sonate:info>
   <sonate:category>
    <rdf:Bag>
      <rdf:li>
        <rdf:Description rdf:about="sonate/Properties/
          Units/SpeedUnit/bps">
         <sonate:name>bps</sonate:name>
         <sonate:info>bits/s</sonate:info>
        </rdf:Description>
      </rdf:li>
      <rdf:li>
        <rdf:Description rdf:about="sonate/Properties/
          Units/SpeedUnit/Kbps">
         <sonate:name>Kbps</sonate:name>
         <sonate:info>Kbits/s</sonate:info>
        </rdf:Description>
      </rdf:li>
      <rdf:li>
        <rdf:Description rdf:about="sonate/Properties/
          Units/SpeedUnit/Mbps">
         <sonate:name>Mbps</sonate:name>
         <sonate:info>Mbits/s</sonate:info>
        </rdf:Description>
      </rdf:li>
      <rdf:li>
        <rdf:Description rdf:about="sonate/Properties/
          Units/SpeedUnit/Gbps">
         <sonate:name>Gbps</sonate:name>
         <sonate:info>Gbits/s</sonate:info>
        </rdf:Description>
```

```
          </rdf:li>
        </rdf:Bag>
      </sonate:category>
    </rdf:Description>
  </rdf:li>
  <rdf:li>
    <rdf:Description rdf:about="sonate/Properties/Units/
        CostUnit">
      <sonate:name>CostUnit</sonate:name>
      <sonate:info>Units for cost</sonate:info>
      <sonate:category>
        <rdf:Bag>
          <rdf:li>
            <rdf:Description rdf:about="sonate/Properties/
                Units/CostUnit/»< sonate : name ></sonate:
                name>
              <sonate:info>Dollar</sonate:info>
            </rdf:Description>
          </rdf:li>
        </rdf:Bag>
      </sonate:category>
    </rdf:Description>
  </rdf:li>
  <rdf:li>
    <rdf:Description rdf:about="sonate/Properties/Units/
        Energy">
      <sonate:name>Energy</sonate:name>
      <sonate:info>Units for energy</sonate:info>
      <sonate:category>
        <rdf:Bag>
          <rdf:li>
            <rdf:Description rdf:about="sonate/Properties/
                Units/Energy/Wh">
              <sonate:name>Wh</sonate:name>
```

```
            <sonate:info>Watt-hour</sonate:info>
          </rdf:Description>
        </rdf:li>
        <rdf:li>
          <rdf:Description rdf:about="sonate/Properties/
             Units/Energy/kWh">
            <sonate:name>kWh</sonate:name>
            <sonate:info>KiloWatt-hour</sonate:info>
          </rdf:Description>
        </rdf:li>
        <rdf:li>
          <rdf:Description rdf:about="sonate/Properties/
             Units/Energy/Ah">
            <sonate:name>Ah</sonate:name>
            <sonate:info>Amp-hour</sonate:info>
          </rdf:Description>
        </rdf:li>
        <rdf:li>
          <rdf:Description rdf:about="sonate/Properties/
             Units/Energy/mAh">
            <sonate:name>mAh</sonate:name>
            <sonate:info>Milliamp-hour</sonate:info>
          </rdf:Description>
        </rdf:li>
      </rdf:Bag>
    </sonate:category>
  </rdf:Description>
        </rdf:li>
      </rdf:Bag>
    </sonate:category>
  </rdf:Description>
</rdf:RDF>
```

A.3 Some Examples of Service Description Using RDF

The dependency description between *Compression* and *Encryption* services
is shown below.

```xml
<?xml version="1.0" encoding="UTF-8"?>
<rdf:RDF xmlns:rdf="http://www.w3.org/1999/02/22-rdf-syntax-ns
    #" xmlns:sonate="http://www.icsy.de/sonate-ns#" xmlns:
    dependency="http://www.icsy.de/sonate-ns#/Properties/
    Dependencies/">
  <rdf:Description rdf:about="dependency/ComEnc">
    <sonate:name>ComEnc</sonate:name>
    <sonate:info>Dependencies between compression and
        encryption services</sonate:info>
    <dependency:Type>Hard</dependency:Type>
    <dependency:Order>Sequence</dependency:Order>
    <sonate:category>
      <rdf:Seq>
        <rdf:li>
          <rdf:Description rdf:about="dependency/Compression">
            <dependency:Target>Service</dependency:Target>
          </rdf:Description>
        </rdf:li>
        <rdf:li>
          <rdf:Description rdf:about="dependency/Encryption">
            <dependency:Target>Service</dependency:Target>
          </rdf:Description>
        </rdf:li>
      </rdf:Seq>
    </sonate:category>
    <dependency:Purpose>Ordering</dependency:Purpose>
  </rdf:Description>
</rdf:RDF>
```

The dependency description between *Negotiation BB* and *Reliable Transmission* service is shown below.

```
<?xml version="1.0" encoding="UTF-8"?>
<rdf:RDF xmlns:rdf="http://www.w3.org/1999/02/22-rdf-syntax-ns
    #" xmlns:sonate="http://www.icsy.de/sonate-ns#" xmlns:
    dependency="http://www.icsy.de/sonate-ns#/Properties/
    Dependencies/">
  <rdf:Description rdf:about="dependency/NegRT">
    <sonate:name>NegRT</sonate:name>
    <sonate:info>Dependencies between "Negotiation" BB and "
        Reliable Transmission" Service</sonate:info>
    <dependency:Type>Hard</dependency:Type>
    <dependency:Order>Unordered</dependency:Order>
    <sonate:category>
      <rdf:Bag>
        <rdf:li>
          <rdf:Description rdf:about="dependency/Negotiation">
            <dependency:Target>BB</dependency:Target>
          </rdf:Description>
        </rdf:li>
        <rdf:li>
          <rdf:Description rdf:about="dependency/
              RealiableTransmission">
            <dependency:Target>Service</dependency:Target>
          </rdf:Description>
        </rdf:li>
      </rdf:Bag>
    </sonate:category>
    <dependency:Purpose>Requirement</dependency:Purpose>
  </rdf:Description>
</rdf:RDF>
```

The dependency description between *Prioritization* and *Authentication and Authorization* BBs is shown as follows

```xml
<?xml version="1.0" encoding="UTF-8"?>
<rdf:RDF xmlns:rdf="http://www.w3.org/1999/02/22-rdf-syntax-ns
    #" xmlns:sonate="http://www.icsy.de/sonate-ns#" xmlns:
    dependency="http://www.icsy.de/sonate-ns#/Properties/
    Dependencies/">
  <rdf:Description rdf:about="dependency/PriorityAAA">
    <sonate:name>PriorityAAA</sonate:name>
    <sonate:info>Dependencies between "Prioritization" BB and
        "Authentication and Authorization" BB</sonate:info>
    <dependency:Type>Hard</dependency:Type>
    <dependency:Order>Sequence</dependency:Order>
    <sonate:category>
      <rdf:Seq>
        <rdf:li>
          <rdf:Description rdf:about="dependency/AAA">
            <dependency:Target>BB</dependency:Target>
          </rdf:Description>
        </rdf:li>
        <rdf:li>
          <rdf:Description rdf:about="dependency/Prioritization
              ">
            <dependency:Target>BB</dependency:Target>
          </rdf:Description>
        </rdf:li>
      </rdf:Seq>
    </sonate:category>
    <dependency:Purpose>Requirement</dependency:Purpose>
  </rdf:Description>
</rdf:RDF>
```

A.4 The XML Schema Of CSDL

The XML schema of the simple version of CSDL is shown in Figure A.1.
This schema is used to describe the capabilities of a building block.

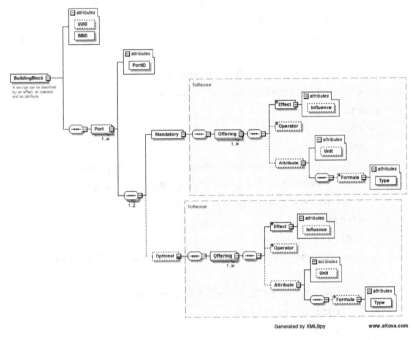

Fig. A.1 An XML Schema to describe the capabilities of a building block

The XML Schema for describing application requirements is shown in
Figure A.2.

A.5 The description of the protocol graph

The XML Schema for describing protocol graphs is shown in Figure A.3.

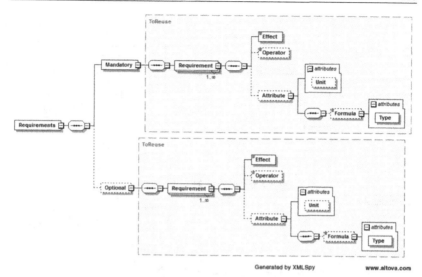

Fig. A.2 An XML Schema to describe application requirements

An example description of a protocol graph is shown below.

```xml
<?xml version="1.0" encoding="UTF-8"?>
<ProtocolGraph xmlns:xsi="http://www.w3.org/2001/XMLSchema-
    instance" xsi:noNamespaceSchemaLocation="
    ProtocolGraphDescription.xsd">
  <Mandatory>
    <Offering>
      <Effect>InOrderDelivery</Effect>
      <Effect>DuplicateControl</Effect>
      <Effect>ErrorDetection</Effect>
      <Effect>LossDetection</Effect>
      <Effect>ErrorCorrection</Effect>
    </Offering>
  </Mandatory>
  <Optional>
    <Offering>
```

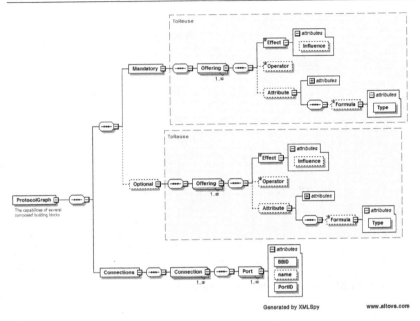

Generated by XMLSpy   www.altova.com

Fig. A.3 An XML Schema to describe the capabilities of protocol graphs

```
    <Effect>PktLossProbability</Effect>
    <Operator>=</Operator>
    <Attribute>
      <Formula Type="value">0</Formula>
    </Attribute>
  </Offering>
</Optional>
<Connections>
  <Connection>
    <Port BBID="SequencingBB" PortID="SequencingBBUp"/>
  </Connection>
  <Connection>
    <Port BBID="SequencingBB" PortID="SequencingBBDown"/>
    <Port BBID="ChecksumBB" PortID="ChecksumBBUp" Influence=
        "Packet"/>
```

```
  </Connection>
  <Connection>
    <Port BBID="ChecksumBB" PortID="ChecksumBBDown"/>
    <Port BBID="GoBackNBB" PortID="GoBackNBBUp"/>
  </Connection>
  <Connection>
    <Port BBID="GoBackNBB" PortID="GoBackNBBDown"/>
  </Connection>
 </Connections>
</ProtocolGraph>
```

A.6 The description of building blocks which represents TCP functionalities

```
<?xml version="1.0" encoding="UTF-8"?>
<BuildingBlock BBID="SequencingBB" xmlns:xsi="http://www.w3.
    org/2001/XMLSchema-instance" xsi:noNamespaceSchemaLocation
    ="descriptionschema.xsd">
  <Port PortID="SequencingBBUp">
    <Mandatory>
      <Offering>
        <Effect>InOrderDelivery</Effect>
        <Operator>=</Operator>
        <Attribute>
          <Formula Type="value">true</Formula>
        </Attribute>
      </Offering>
      <Offering>
        <Effect>DuplicateControl</Effect>
        <Operator>=</Operator>
        <Attribute>
```

```xml
      <Formula Type="value">true</Formula>
    </Attribute>
  </Offering>
 </Mandatory>
</Port>
</BuildingBlock>


<?xml version="1.0" encoding="UTF-8"?>
<BuildingBlock BBID="ChecksumBB" xmlns:xsi="http://www.w3.org
   /2001/XMLSchema-instance"
xsi:noNamespaceSchemaLocation="descriptionschema.xsd">
  <Port PortID="ChecksumBBUp">
   <Mandatory>
    <Offering>
       <Effect Influence="All">ErrorDetection
       </Effect>
       <Operator>=</Operator>
       <Attribute><Formula Type="value">true</Formula>
       </Attribute>
     </Offering>
   </Mandatory>
  </Port>
</BuildingBlock>


<?xml version="1.0" encoding="UTF-8"?>
<BuildingBlock BBID="GoBackNBB"
xmlns:xsi="http://www.w3.org/2001/XMLSchema-instance" xsi:
   noNamespaceSchemaLocation="descriptionschema.xsd">
  <Port PortID="GoBackNBBUp">
   <Optional>
     <Offering>
       <Effect>PktLossProbability</Effect>
       <Operator>=</Operator>
```

```
    <Attribute>
      <Formula Type="value">0</Formula>
    </Attribute>
    </Offering>
  </Optional>
  <Mandatory>
    <Offering>
      <Effect>LossDetection</Effect>
      <Operator>=</Operator>
      <Attribute>
          <Formula Type="value">true</Formula>
      </Attribute>
    </Offering>
    <Offering>
      <Effect>ErrorCorrection</Effect>
      <Operator>=</Operator>
      <Attribute>
          <Formula Type="value">true</Formula>
      </Attribute>
    </Offering>
  </Mandatory>
  </Port>
</BuildingBlock>
```

A.7 Examples of Building Blocks Using CSDL

The description of an *encryption* building block AES256 is shown below

```
<?xml version="1.0" encoding="UTF-8"?>
<BuildingBlock BBID="aes256" xmlns:xsi="http://www.w3.org
    /2001/XMLSchema-instance" xsi:noNamespaceSchemaLocation="
    descriptionschema.xsd">
    <Port PortID="aes256Up">
    <Mandatory>
```

```
<Offering>
  <Effect>Encryption</Effect>
  <Operator>=</Operator>
  <Attribute>
      <Formula Type="value">true</Formula>
  </Attribute>
</Offering>
</Mandatory>
<Optional>
  <Offering>
    <Effect>Encryption</Effect>
    <Operator>=</Operator>
    <Attribute Unit="bit">
        <Formula Type="value">256</Formula>
    </Attribute>
  </Offering>
</Optional>
</Port>
</BuildingBlock>
```

The description of a *CRC-32* building block is shown below

```
<?xml version="1.0" encoding="UTF-8"?>
<BuildingBlock BBID="crc32"
xmlns:xsi="http://www.w3.org/2001/XMLSchema-instance" xsi:
    noNamespaceSchemaLocation="descriptionschema.xsd">
  <Port PortID="crc32Up">
    <Mandatory>
      <Offering>
        <Effect>ErrorDetection</Effect>
        <Operator>=</Operator>
        <Attribute>
            <Formula Type="value">true</Formula>
        </Attribute>
      </Offering>
```

```
    </Mandatory>
    <Optional>
     <Offering>
       <Effect>ErrorDetection</Effect>
       <Operator>&lt;=</Operator>
       <Attribute Unit="bit">
           <Formula Type="value">8</Formula>
       </Attribute>
     </Offering>
    </Optional>
   </Port>
</BuildingBlock>
```

The description of a four dimensional *Parity Check* building block is shown below

```
<?xml version="1.0" encoding="UTF-8"?>
<BuildingBlock BBID="fourdimentionalparitycheck" xmlns:xsi="
    http://www.w3.org/2001/XMLSchema-instance" xsi:
    noNamespaceSchemaLocation="descriptionschema.xsd">
  <Port PortID="fourdimentionalparitycheckUp">
   <Mandatory>
     <Offering>
       <Effect>ErrorCorrection</Effect>
       <Operator>=</Operator>
       <Attribute>
           <Formula Type="value">true</Formula>
       </Attribute>
     </Offering>
     <Offering>
       <Effect>ErrorDetection</Effect>
       <Operator>=</Operator>
       <Attribute>
           <Formula Type="value">true</Formula>
```

```
         </Attribute>
       </Offering>
     </Mandatory>
     <Optional>
       <Offering>
         <Effect>ErrorCorrection</Effect>
         <Operator>&lt;=</Operator>
         <Attribute Unit="bit">
             <Formula Type="value">2</Formula>
         </Attribute>
       </Offering>
       <Offering>
         <Effect>ErrorDetection</Effect>
         <Operator>&lt;=</Operator>
         <Attribute Unit="bit">
             <Formula Type="value">2</Formula>
         </Attribute>
       </Offering>
     </Optional>
   </Port>
</BuildingBlock>
```

The description of a *HammingCode* building block is shown below

```
<?xml version="1.0" encoding="UTF-8"?>
<BuildingBlock BBID="hammingcode" xmlns:xsi="http://www.w3.org
    /2001/XMLSchema-instance" xsi:noNamespaceSchemaLocation="
    descriptionschema.xsd">
  <Port PortID="hammingcodeUp">
    <Mandatory>
      <Offering>
        <Effect>ErrorDetection</Effect>
        <Operator>=</Operator>
        <Attribute>
            <Formula Type="value">true</Formula>
```

```
      </Attribute>
    </Offering>
    <Offering>
      <Effect>ErrorCorrection</Effect>
      <Operator>=</Operator>
      <Attribute>
          <Formula Type="value">true</Formula>
      </Attribute>
    </Offering>
  </Mandatory>
  <Optional>
    <Offering>
      <Effect>ErrorDetection</Effect>
      <Operator>&lt;=</Operator>
      <Attribute Unit="bit">
          <Formula Type="value">2</Formula>
      </Attribute>
    </Offering>
    <Offering>
      <Effect>ErrorCorrection</Effect>
      <Operator>&lt;=</Operator>
      <Attribute Unit="bit">
          <Formula Type="value">1</Formula>
      </Attribute>
    </Offering>
  </Optional>
  </Port>
</BuildingBlock>
```

The description of *IPv6* building block is given below

```
<?xml version="1.0" encoding="UTF-8"?>
<BuildingBlock BBID="ipv6" xmlns:xsi="http://www.w3.org/2001/
    XMLSchema-instance" xsi:noNamespaceSchemaLocation="
    descriptionschema.xsd">
```

```
<Port PortID="ipv6Up">
  <Mandatory>
    <Offering>
      <Effect>Addressing</Effect>
      <Operator>=</Operator>
      <Attribute>
          <Formula Type="value">true</Formula>
      </Attribute>
    </Offering>
  </Mandatory>
  <Optional>
    <Offering>
      <Effect>Addressing</Effect>
      <Operator>=</Operator>
      <Attribute Unit="bit">
          <Formula Type="value">128</Formula>
      </Attribute>
    </Offering>
    <Offering>
      <Effect>MaxPacketSize</Effect>
      <Operator>=</Operator>
      <Attribute Unit="byte">
          <Formula Type="value">65535</Formula>
      </Attribute>
    </Offering>
  </Optional>
</Port>
</BuildingBlock>
```

The description of a *Retransmission* building block is given below

```
<?xml version="1.0" encoding="UTF-8"?>
<BuildingBlock BBID="retransmission"
xmlns:xsi="http://www.w3.org/2001/XMLSchema-instance"
xsi:noNamespaceSchemaLocation="descriptionschema.xsd">
```

```xml
<Port PortID="retransmissionUp">
  <Mandatory>
    <Offering>
      <Effect>LossDetection</Effect>
      <Operator>=</Operator>
      <Attribute>
          <Formula Type="value">true</Formula>
      </Attribute>
    </Offering>
  </Mandatory>
  <Optional>
    <Offering>
      <Effect>DataRate</Effect>
      <Operator>=</Operator>
      <Attribute Unit="bit/s">
        <Formula Type="python">if retransmitpacket == 1:
            DataRate = DataRate + (PacketSize/Time) else:
            DataRate</Formula>
      </Attribute>
    </Offering>
  </Optional>
</Port>
</BuildingBlock>
```

List of References

1. Netlet-based node architecture (nena). http://nena.intend-net.org/. URL http://nena.intend-net.org/. Online; accessed 30-April-2012
2. Network simulator (ns). http://www.isi.edu/nsnam/ns/. URL http://www.isi.edu/nsnam/ns/. Online; accessed 29-May-2012
3. open wireless network simulator (openwns). http://www.openwns.org/. URL http://www.openwns.org/. Online; accessed 29-May-2012
4. Standardization candidate from itu kleidoscope 2013. http://www.itu.int/en/ITU-T/academia/kaleidoscope/2013/Documents/Presentations/K-2013_Wrap-up%20Session.pdf. URL http://www.itu.int/en/ITU-T/academia/kaleidoscope/2013/Documents/Presentations/K-2013_Wrap-up%20Session.pdf
5. 25010:2011, I.: Systems and software engineering – systems and software quality requirements and evaluation (square) – system and software quality models. ISO/IEC Standard (2011). URL http://www.iso.org/iso/home/store/catalogue_ics/catalogue_detail_ics.htm?csnumber=35733
6. 4ward eu project. http://www.4ward-project.eu/. URL http://www.4ward-project.eu/. Online; accessed 25-April-2011
7. Abbott, M.B., Peterson, L.L.: A language-based approach to protocol implementation. In: ACM SIGCOMM Computer Communication Review, vol. 22, pp. 27–38 (1992)
8. Allman, M., Praxson, V.: TCP Congestion Control. http://tools.ietf.org/html/rfc5681 (2009). URL http://tools.ietf.org/html/rfc5681. RFC 5681
9. Autonomic network architecture (ana). www.ana-project.org. URL www.ana-project.org. Online; accessed 25-April-2011
10. Anderson, D.P.: Automated protocol implementation with rtag. IEEE Transactions on Software Engineering 14(3), 291–300 (1988)
11. Autoi project. URL http://ist-autoi.eu/autoi/. Online; accessed 15-April-2010
12. Bagnulo, M., Matthews, P., van Beijnum, I.: Stateful nat64: Network address and protocol translation from ipv6 clients to ipv4 servers. http://www.ietf.org/rfc/rfc6146.txt (2011). URL http://www.ietf.org/rfc/rfc6146.txt. RFC 6146 (Proposed Standard)

13. Baldine, I., Vellala, M., Wang, A., Rouskas, G.N., Dutta, R., Stevenson, D.S.: A unified software architecture to enable cross-layer design in the future internet. In: 6th International Conference on Future Internet Technologies, pp. 26–32 (2007)

14. Baldwin, C.Y., Clark, K.B.: Design Rules, Vol. 1: The Power of Modularity, first edn. The MIT Press (2000)

15. Banks, J.: Handbook of Simulation Principles, Methodology, Advances, Applications, and Practice. Engineering and Management Press (1998)

16. Bao, C., Huitema, C., Bagnulo, M., Boucadair, M., Li, X.: Ipv6 addressing of ipv4/ipv6 translators. http://www.ietf.org/rfc/rfc6052.txt (2010). URL http://www.ietf.org/rfc/rfc6052.txt. RFC 6052 (Proposed Standard)

17. Bhatti, N.T., Schlichting, R.D.: A system for constructing configurable high-level protocols. In: SIGCOMM '95 Proceedings of the Conference on Applications, Technologies, Architectures, and Protocols for Computer Communication, vol. 25, pp. 138–150 (1995)

18. Biagioni, E.: A structured tcp in standard ml. In: SIGCOMM '94 Proceedings of the conference on Communications architectures, protocols and applications, vol. 24, pp. 36–45 (1994)

19. Bolognesi, T., Brinksma, E.: Introduction to the iso specification language lotos. Computer Networks and ISDN Systems - Special Issue: Protocol Specification and Testing 14(1), 25–59 (1987)

20. Bourner, T.: The research process: Four step to success. In T. Greenfield (Ed.), Research methods: Guidance for postgraduates (1996)

21. BOUSSINOT, F., SIMONE, R.D.: The esterel language. PROCEEDINGS OF THE IEEE 79(7), 1293–1304 (1991)

22. Box, D.F., Schmidt, D.C., Suda, T.: Adaptive: An object-oriented framework for flexible and adaptive communication protocols. In: Proceedings of the IFIP TC6/WG6.4 Fourth International Conference on High Performance Networking IV, North-Holland Publishing Co. Amsterdam, The Netherlands, pp. 367–382. Liege, Belgium (1992)

23. Best paper award candidates for nof 2011. http://phare.lip6.fr/nof2011/index.php?page=info. URL http://phare.lip6.fr/nof2011/index.php?page=info. Online; accessed 27-September-2014

24. Braden, R., Clark, D., Shenker, S., Wroclawski, J.: Developing a next-generation internet architecture. ISI White Paper, DARPA (2000)

25. Braden, R., Faber, T., Handley, M.: From protocol stack to protocol heap: role-based architecture. SIGCOMM Computer Communication Review 33(1), 17–22 (2003). DOI http://doi.acm.org/10.1145/774763.774765

26. Brooks, A., Kaupp, T., Makarenko, A., Williams, S., Orebäck, A.: Towards component-based robotics. In: IEEE/RSJ International Conference on Intelligent Robots and Systems, pp. 163 – 168 (2005)

27. Canfora, G., Penta, M.D., Esposito, R., Villani, M.L.: An approach for qos-aware service composition based on genetic algorithms. 2005 conference on Genetic and evolutionary computation pp. 1069 – 1075 (2005)

28. Casado, M.: Architectural Support for Security Management in Enterprize Networks. PhD Dissertation, Stanford University (2007)

29. Commission, E.: Ibm application analysis, research and development in advanced communication technologies in europe. Technical report r1071, European Commission (1991)

30. DARPA: Transmission Control Protocol. http://www.ietf.org/rfc/rfc793.txt (1981). URL http://www.ietf.org/rfc/rfc793.txt. RFC 793

31. Deering, S., Hinden, R.: Internet Protocol, Version 6 (IPv6) Specification. https://www.ietf.org/rfc/rfc2460.txt (1998). URL https://www.ietf.org/rfc/rfc2460.txt. RFC 2460

32. Dutta, R., Rouskas, G., Baldine, I., Bragg, A., Stevenson, D.: The silo architecture for services integration, control, and optimization for the future internet. In: ICC '07. IEEE International Conference on Communications, 2007, pp. 1899 – 1904 (2007)

33. Dutta, R., Rouskas, G.N., Baldine, I., Bragg, A., Stevenson, D.: The silo architecture for services integration, control, and optimization for the future internet. In: IEEE ICC, pp. 24–27 (2007)

34. Ehrgott, M., Gandibleux, X.: Multiple criteria optimization - state of the art annotated bibliographic surveys. Kluwer Academic Publishers (2003)

35. Erl, T.: Service-Oriented Architecture. Prentice Hall (2006)

36. Erl, T.: SOA Design Patterns. Prentice Hall (2008)

37. Feamster, N., Gao, L., Rexford, J.: How to lease the internet in your spare time. ACM SIGCOMM Computer Communication Review **37**(1), 61 – 64 (2007)

38. Future internet engineering. https://www.iip.net.pl/. URL https://www.iip.net.pl/. Online; accessed 02-October-2013

39. Fiedler, M., Hossfeld, T., Tran-Gia, P.: A general quantitative relationship between quality of experience and quality of service. IEEE Network: The Magazine of Global Internetworking - Special issue on improving quality of experience for network services **24**(2), 36–41 (2010)

40. Future internet design (find). http://www.nets-find.net/. URL http://www.nets-find.net/. Online; accessed 02-October-2014

41. Forwarding on gates. http://www.tu-ilmenau.de/en/integrated-communication-systems-group/research/projects/g-lab-fog/. URL http://www.tu-ilmenau.de/en/integrated-communication-systems-group/research/projects/g-lab-fog/. Online; accessed 25-April-2011

42. Foundation, E.F.: Cracking DES Secrets of Encryption Research, Wiretap Politics & Chip Design, first edn. O'Reilly Media (1998)

43. Rahamatullah khondoker, talk in a research seminar titled: Service composition and selection in a service oriented network architecture, karlsruhe institute of technology, 26 oct 2010, karlsruhe, germany. http://telematics.tm.kit.edu/downloads/ForSem_2010_10_26_KHONDOKER.pptx. URL http://telematics.tm.kit.edu/downloads/ForSem_2010_10_26_KHONDOKER.pptx. Online; accessed 05-December-2012

44. Ganapathy, S., Wolf, T.: Design of a network service architecture. In: Proc. of Sixteenth IEEE International Conference on Computer Communications and Networks (ICCCN). Honolulu, Hawaii (2007)

45. Geppert, B., Roessler, F.: Generic engineering of communication protocols - current experience and future issues. In: ICFEM '97: Proceedings of the 1st International

Conference on Formal Engineering Methods, p. 70. IEEE Computer Society, Washington, DC, USA (1997)

46. German lab (g-lab). http://www.german-lab.de/. URL http://www.german-lab.de/. Online; accessed 11-October-2012

47. German lab (g-lab) phase 1. http://www.german-lab.de/phase-1/. URL http://www.german-lab.de/phase-1/. Online; accessed 11-October-2012

48. Günther, D., Schwerdel, D., Siddiqui, A., Khondoker, R., Müller, P.: Poster presentation for the demo: Selecting and composing requirement aware protocol graphs with sonate. In: Proceedings of the 12th Würzburg Workshop on IP: Joint ITG, ITC, and EuroNF Workshop on "Visions of Future Generation Networks" EuroView 2012 (2012)

49. Günther, D., Schwerdel, D., Siddiqui, A., Khondoker, R., Müller, P.: Selecting and composing requirement aware protocol graphs with sonate. In: Proceedings of the 12th Würzburg Workshop on IP: Joint ITG, ITC, and EuroNF Workshop on "Visions of Future Generation Networks" EuroView 2012 (2012)

50. Günther, D., Veith, E.M., Müller, P.: A way to identify decision criteria for selecting different mechanisms which provide reliable transmission in a future internet architecture. In: 2011 7th EURO-NGI Conference on Next Generation Internet (NGI), pp. 1 – 6 (2011)

51. Haas, Z.: A protocol structure for high-speed communication over broadband isdn. IEEE Network Magazine pp. 64–70 (1991)

52. Han, D., Anand, A., Dogar, F., Li, B., Lim, H., Machado, M., Mukundan, A., Wu, W., Akella, A., Andersen, D.G., Byers, J.W., Seshan, S., Steenkiste, P.: Xia: Efficient support for evolvable internetworking. In: 9th USENIX Symposium on Networked Systems Design and Implementation (NSDI-12), pp. 1 – 14 (2012)

53. Hanka, O., Wippel, H.: Secure deployment of application-tailored protocols in future networks. In: Proceedings of the Second International Conference on the Network of the Future (NoF 2011), pp. 10–14 (2011)

54. Henke, C., Siddiqui, A., Khondoker, R.: Network functional composition: State of the art. 2010 Australasian Telecommunication Networks and Application Conference, Auckland, New Zealand pp. 43 – 48 (2010)

55. Hinloopen, E.: De regime methode, ma thesis. Interfaculty Actuariat and Econometrics, Free University Amsterdam (1985)

56. Holzinger, A.: Usability engineering methods for software developers. Communications of the ACM - Interaction design and children 48(1), 71–74 (2005)

57. Hutchinson, N.C., Peterson, L.L.: The x-kernel: An architecture for implementing network protocols. IEEE Transactions on Software Engineering 17(1), 64–76 (1991)

58. Hutchinson, N.C., Peterson, L.L., Abbott, M.B., OMalley, S.: Rpc in the x-kernel: Evaluating new design techniques. In: SOSP '89 Proceedings of the twelfth ACM symposium on Operating systems principles, pp. 91–101 (1989)

59. Investigating rina as an alternative to tcp/ip. http://irati.eu/. URL http://irati.eu/. Online; accessed 02-October-2014

60. ITU-T: Common management services - state management - protocol neutral requirements and analysis. Recommendation M.3701, International Telecommunication Union, Geneva (2010)

61. ITU-T: ITU-T Recommendation Y.1541: Network performance objectives for ip-based services. Geneva (2011)
62. Keller, A., Hossmann, T., May, M., Bouabene, G., Jelger, C., Tschudin, C.: A system architecture for evolving protocol stacks. In: Proceedings of 17th International Conference on Computer Communications and Networks, 2008, pp. 1 – 7. IEEE (2008)
63. Keller, A., Hossmann, T., May, M., Bourabene, G., Jelger, C., Tschudin, C.: A system architecture for evolving protocol stacks. In: ICCCN 08) (2007)
64. Kenny, R.L., Raiffa, H.: Decisions with mulitple objectives: Preferences and value trade-offs. John Wiley and Sons, New York (1976)
65. Khondoker, R., Reuther, B., Müller, P.: Selecting communication services in a service oriented network architecture. In: Proceedings of 10th Würzburg Workshop on IP: Joint ITG, ITC, and EuroNF Workshop on "Visions of Future Generation Networks" EuroView 2010 (2010)
66. Khondoker, R., Reuther, B., Schwerdel, D., Siddiqui, A., Müller, P.: Describing and selecting communication services in a service oriented network architecture. In: the proceedings of the 2011 ITU-T Kleidoscope event, Beyond the Internet? Innovations for future networks and services, Pune, India (2010)
67. Khondoker, R., Siddique, A., Reuther, B., Müller, P.: Service orientation paradigm in future network architectures. In: 2012 Sixth International Conference on Innovative Mobile and Internet Services in Ubiquitous Computing (IMIS), Palermo, Italy, pp. 346 – 351 (2012)
68. Khondoker, R., Veith, E.M., Müller, P.: A description language for communication services of future network architectures. In Proceedings of the 2011 International Conference on the Network of the Future pp. 69 – 76 (2011)
69. Kim, E., Lee, Y., Kim, Y., Park, H., Kim, J., Moon, B., Yun, J., Kang, G.: Web services quality factors version 1.0. Candidate OASIS Standard 01 (2012). URL http://docs.oasis-open.org/wsqm/WS-Quality-Factors/v1.0/WS-Quality-Factors-v1.0.pdf
70. Kitchenham, B.: Procedures for performing systematic reviews. Tech. rep., Joint Technical Reports of Keele University Technical Report TR/SE-0401 and NICTA Technical Report 0400011T.1, Keele University and NICTA (2004)
71. Kohler, E., Kaashoek, M.F., R.Monotgomery, D.: A readable tcp in the prolac protocol language. In: SIGCOMM '99 Proceedings of the conference on Applications, technologies, architectures, and protocols for computer communication and ACM SIGCOMM Computer Communication Review, vol. 29, pp. 3–13 (1999)
72. Liers, F., Volkert, T., Martin, D., Backhaus, H., Wippel, H., Veith, E.M., Siddiqui, A.A., Khondoker, R.: Gapi: A g-lab application-to-network interface. In Proceedings of the 11th Würzburg Workshop on IP: Joint ITG and Euro-NF Workshop on "Visions of Future Generation Networks" (EuroView 2011) (2011)
73. Liers, F., Volkert, T., Mitschele-Thiel, A.: Scalable network support for application requirements with forwarding on gates. In: Proceedings of 11th Würzburg Workshop on IP: Joint ITG and Euro-NF Workshop "Visions of Future Generation Networkse" (EuroView2011) (2011)

74. Liers, F., Volkert, T., Mitschele-Thiel, A.: The forwarding on gates architecture: Merging intserv and diffserv. In: Proceedings of International Conference on Advances in Future Internet (AFIN 2012) (2012)

75. Martin, D., Völker, L., Zitterbart, M.: A flexible framework for future internet design, assessment, and operation. Computer Networks **55**(4), 910–918 (2011)

76. Matsui, M.: Linear Cryptanalysis method for DES Cipher. Springer-Verlag (1998)

77. Matsumoto, Y.: Some experiences in promoting reusable software: Presentation in higher abstract levels. IEEE Transactions in Software Engineering **SE-10**(5), 502 – 513 (1984)

78. Milanovic, N., Malek, M.: Current solutions for web service composition. IEEE INTERNET COMPUTING pp. 51 – 59 (2004)

79. de Montis, A., Toro, P.D., Droste-Franke, B., Omann, I., Stagl, S.: Assessing the quality of different mcda methods (2000)

80. Moore, G.E.: Cramming More Components onto Integrated Circuits. Electronics Magazine (1965)

81. Müller, P., Reuther, B.: Future internet architecture - a service oriented approach (future internet architecture - ein serviceorientierter ansatz). it - Information Technology **50**(6), 383–389 (2008)

82. Müller, P., Reuther, B.: Future internet architecture - a service oriented approach (future internet architecture - ein serviceorientierter ansatz). it - Information Technology **50**(6), 383–389 (2008)

83. Munda, G.: Multi criteria evaluation in a fuzzy environment - theory and applications in ecological economics. Hidelberg: Physika Verlag (1995)

84. Nsf future internet architecture project. http://www.nets-fia.net/. URL http://www.nets-fia.net/. Online; accessed 02-October-2014

85. Nielson, J.: Usability Engineering. Morgan Kaufmann (1994)

86. Oberle, D., Barros, A., Kylau, U., Heinzl, S.: A unified description language for human to automated services. Information Systems **38**(1), 155 – 181 (2013)

87. O'Malley, S.W., Peterson, L.L.: A dynamic network architecture. ACM Transactions on Computer Systems **10**(2), 110–143 (1992)

88. OMALLEY, S.W., PETERSON, L.L.: A dynamic network architecture. ACM Transactions on Computer Systems **10**(2), 110–143 (1992)

89. Papazoglou, M.P.: Service-oriented computing: Concepts, characteristics and directions. In: WISE 2003, Roma, Italy, pp. 3–12 (2003)

90. Parnas, D.L., Clements, P.C., Weiss, D.M.: Software reusability: vol. 1, concepts and models. ACM (1989)

91. Peterson, L., Shenker, S., Turner, J.: Overcoming the internet impasse through virtualization. Computer **38**(4), 34 – 41 (2005)

92. Popien, C., Meyer, B.: A service request description language. In: Seventh International Conference on Formal Description Techniques, pp. 4–7 (1994)

93. Porta, T.F.L., Schwartz, M.: Architecture, features, and implementation of high-speed transport protocols. IEEE Network Magazine pp. 14 – 22 (1991)

94. Pressman, R.S.: Software Engineering A Practitioner's Approach, 5th edn. McGraw-Hill Higher Education (2000)

95. Recommendations: Ccitt recommendations 1.211: B-isdn service aspects (1991)

96. Reuther, B.: Ein serviceorientierter ansatz zur abstraktion von kommunikationsprotokollen im internet). Ph.D. thesis, Department of Computer Science, University of Kaiserslautern (2010)
97. Reuther, B., Henrici, D.: A model for service-oriented communication systems. Systems Architecture **54**(6), 594–606 (2008)
98. Recursive internetwork architecture. http://csr.bu.edu/rina/. URL http://csr.bu.edu/rina/. Online; accessed 03-February-2012
99. Roy, B.: Multiple criteria methodology for decision aiding. Parigi: Economica (1985)
100. Saaty, T.L.: The analytic hierarchy process. McGraw-Hill, New York (1980)
101. Saaty, T.L.: Decision making with the analytic hierarchy process. Int. J. Services Sciences **1**(1), 83–98 (2008)
102. Schmidt, D.C., Box, D.F., Suda, T.: Adaptive: a flexible and adaptive transport system architecture to support lightweight protocols for multimedia applications on high-speed networks. In: Proceedings of the First International Symposium on High-Performance Distributed Computing (HPDC-1), pp. 174–186 (1992)
103. Schmidt, D.C., Box, D.F., Suda, T.: Adaptive: A dynamically assembled protocol transformation, integration, and evaluation environment. Concurrency: Practice and Experience **5**, 269–286 (1993)
104. Schmidt, D.C., Box, D.F., Suda, T.: Adaptive: A dynamically assembled protocol transformation, integration, and evaluation environment. Concurrency: Practice and Experience **5**, 269–286 (1993)
105. Schwerdel, D., Günther, D., Khondoker, R., Reuther, B., Müller, P.: A building block interaction model for flexible future internet architectures. In: Proceedings of Next Generation Internet 2011, Kaiserslautern, Germany, pp. 1 – 8 (2011)
106. Schwerdel, D., Hock, D., Günther, D., Reuther, B., Tran-Gia, P., Müller, P.: Tomato - a network experimentation tool. In: 7th International Conference on Testbeds and Research Infrastructures for the Development of Networks and Communities (TridentCom 2011), Shanghai, China, pp. 1 –10 (2011)
107. Schwerdel, D., Reuther, B., Müller, P.: On using evolutionary algorithms for solving the functional composition problem. In: 10th Würzburg Workshop on IP: Joint ITG, and EuroNF Workshop on 'Visions of Future Generation Networks' EuroView 2010 (2010)
108. Selfnet project. www.ict-selfnet.eu. URL www.ict-selfnet.eu. Online; accessed 10-July-2007
109. Siddiqui, A., Khondoker, R., Müller, P.: Template based composition for requirements based network stack. In: ATNAC'12: Proceedings of Australasian Telecommunication Networks and Application Conference, Brisbane, Australia, pp. 1 – 6 (2012)
110. Siddiqui, A., Khondoker, R., Reuther, B., Müller, P., Henke, C., Backhaus, H.: Functional composition and its challenges. In: 2011 Fifth International Conference on Innovative Mobile and Internet Services in Ubiquitous Computing (IMIS), Seoul, South Korea, pp. 336 – 340 (2011)
111. Srinivasan, S., Woo, J., Eric, L., Kester, L., Schulzrinne, H., Hilt, V., Seetharaman, S., Khan, A.: Netserv: Dynamically deploying in-network services. In: ReArch'09: Proceedings of the 2009 Workshop on Re-architecting the Internet, pp. 1–6. ACM, New York, USA (2009). DOI http://doi.acm.org/10.1145/1658978.1658988

112. Srisuresh, P., Egevang, K.: Traditional ip network address translator (traditional nat). http://www.ietf.org/rfc/rfc3022.txt (2001). URL http://www.ietf.org/rfc/rfc3022.txt. RFC 3022 (Informational)

113. Stallings, W.: Data and Computer Communications, Fifth Edition. Springer (2003)

114. Stallings, W.: Data and Computer Communications, Fifth Edition. Prentice Hall (2006)

115. Stankiewicz, R., Cholda, P., Jajszczyk, A.: Qox: What is it really. IEEE Communications Magazine 49(4), 148 – 158 (2011)

116. Steinmetz, R., Nahrstedt, K.: Multimedia Systems. Springer (2004)

117. Stevens, W.R.: TCP/IP Illustrated, Volume 1: The Protocols, vol. 1. Addison-Wesley (1994)

118. Stevens, W.R.: TCP/IP Illustrated, Volume 2: The Implementation, vol. 2. Addison-Wesley (1995)

119. Stewart, R.: Stream Control Transmission Protocol. http://tools.ietf.org/html/rfc4960 (2007). URL http://tools.ietf.org/html/rfc4960. RFC 4960

120. Stiller, B.: Fukss: Ein funktionsbasiertes kommunikationssubsystem zur flexiblen konfiguration von kommunikationsprotokollen. GI/ITG-Fachgruppe Kommunikation und Verteilte Systeme (1994)

121. Tanenbaum, A.S., Wetherall, D.J.: Computer Networks, 5th Edition. Prentice Hall (2003)

122. Touch, J.D., Pingali, V.K.: The rna metaprotocol. In: ICCCN 2008, pp. 157–162 (2008)

123. Touch, J.D., Wang, Y.S., Pingali, V.: A recursive network architecture. Tech. Rep. isi-tr-2006-626, USC/ISI, 4676 Admiralty Way, Marina del Rey, CA 90266 USA (2006). Online; accessed 25-April-2011

124. Touch, J.D., Wang, Y.S., Pingali, V.: A recursive network architecture. http://www.isi.edu/touch/pubs/isi-tr-2006-626/ (2006). URL http://www.isi.edu/touch/pubs/isi-tr-2006-626/. Online; accessed 25-April-2011

125. Tschudin, C.: Flexible protocol stacks. ACM SIGCOMM Computer Communication Review 21(4), 197–205 (1991)

126. Tschudin, C., Hold, R.: Network pointers. ACM SIGCOMM Computer Communications Review 33, 23–28 (2003)

127. Tschudin, C., Jelger, C.: An "autonomic network architecture" research project. Praxis der Informationsverarbeitung und Kommunikation (PIK Magazine) pp. 26 – 31 (2007)

128. Turner, K.J.: Using Formal Description Techniques - An Introduction to Estelle, LOTOS and SDL. John Wiley and Sons Ltd. (1993)

129. Vogt, M., Plagemann, T., Plattner, B., Walter, T.: Eine laufzeitumgebung fdacapo. GI/ITG-Arbeitstreffen Verteilte Multimedia-Systeme (1993)

130. Vogt, M., Plagemann, T., Plattner, B., Walter, T.: A run-time environment for da capo. In: Proceedings of INET93 International Networking Conference of the Internet Society (1993)

131. Volker, L., Martin, D., El Khayaut, I., Werle, C., Zitterbart, M.: A node architecture for 1000 future networks. In: IEEE International Conference on Communications 2009 (ICC 2009), pp. 1 –5 (2009). DOI 10.1109/ICCW.2009.5207996

132. Völker, L., Martin, D., Khayat, I.E., Werle, C., Zitterbart, M.: A node architecture for 1000 future networks. In: International Workshop on the Network of the Future 2009, Dresden, Germany (2009)

133. Völker, L., Martin, D., Werle, C., Zitterbart, M., Khayat, I.E.: Selecting concurrent network architectures at runtime. In: IEEE International Conference on Communications (ICC 2009) (2009)

134. Völker, L., Werle, C., Zitterbart, M.: Decision process for automated selection of security protocols. In: 33rd IEEE Conference on Local Computer Networks (LCN 2008), Montreal, Canada, pp. 223 – 229 (2008)

135. Volkert, T., Liers, F.: Video transcoding and rerouting in forwarding on gates networks. In: Proceedings of the 12th Würzburg Workshop on IP: Joint ITG, ITC, and EuroNF Workshop on "Visions of Future Generation Networks" EuroView 2012 (2012)

136. Voogd, H.: Multi-criteria analysis with mixed qualitative-quantitative data. Delft University of Technology, Department of Urban and Regional Planning (1981)

137. W3CRecommendation: Owl 2 web ontology language document overview, w3c recommendation, 27 october 2009

138. W3CRecommendation: Rdf/xml syntax specification (revised), w3c recommendation, 10 february 2004

139. W3CRecommendation: Web services description language (wsdl) version 2.0, part 1: Core language, w3c recommendation, 26 june 2007

140. Wang, Y.S., Touch, J.D., Silvester, J.A.: A unified model for end point resolution and domain conversion for multi-hop, multi-layer communication (2004). URL http://www.isi.edu/touch/pubs/isi-tr-2004-590/. Online; accessed 25-April-2011

141. Warrier, U., Relan, P., Berry, O., Bannister, J.: A network management language for osi networks. In: SIGCOMM '88 Symposium proceedings on Communications architectures and protocols, vol. 18, pp. 98–105. ACM (1988)

142. Welzl, S., Jorer, S., Gjessing, S.: Towards a protocol-independent internet transport api. In: IEEE International Conference on Communications (ICC 2011). Kyoto, Japan (2011)

143. expressive internet architecture. http://www.cs.cmu.edu/~xia/technical/technical-approach.html. URL http://www.cs.cmu.edu/~xia/technical/technical-approach.html. Online; accessed 3-Feb-2012

144. Zimmermann, H.: Osi reference model - the iso model of architecture for open systems interconnection. IEEE Transactions on Communications 28(4), 425 – 432 (1980)

145. Zitterbart, M., Stiller, B.: A concept for a flexible high performance transport system. Telecommunications and Multimedia Applications in Computer Science pp. 365 – 374 (1991)

Printed in the United States
By Bookmasters